No Kidding

NO KIDDING

Women Writers on
Bypassing Parenthood

foreword by **Jennifer Coolidge**

edited by **Henriette Mantel**

SEAL

To Sarah, Holly, Daniel, Paige, Grace, Julianna, Kaleena, and Jaydon:
Thanks for being the kids I didn't have.

—Henriette Mantel

Seal Press
A Member of the Perseus Books Group
1700 Fourth Street
Berkeley, California 94710

Library of Congress Cataloging-in-Publication Data

No kidding : women writers on bypassing parenthood / [edited] by
Henriette
Mantel.
    p. cm.
  ISBN 978-1-58005-443-0
1. Childlessness. 2. Parenthood. 3. Families. 4. Choice (Psychology)
I. Mantel, Henriette.
  HQ755.8.N596 2013
  306.87--dc23
                              2012037431

10 9 8 7 6 5 4 3 2 1

Cover design by Daniel Pelavin
Interior design by Kate Basart

Printed in the United States of America
Distributed by Publishers Group West

Contents

Foreword

Jennifer Coolidge

I met Henriette Mantel in 1994, when we were both cast in a short-lived sketch show for ABC called *She TV*. She was the first person I met in Los Angeles who was a true nonconformist—a breath of fresh air and a fellow New Englander who didn't edit herself. I fell hard for Henriette when she did this hilarious stand-up bit called, "Pretty, Pretty, Pretty," in which she laments the lack of substance in Hollywood and that talent is no longer a necessity. Way ahead of her time, she unconsciously predicted this whole Kardashian debacle. It's not about anything anymore, it's just about being pretty.

We have always managed to stay loosely connected. At one point she generously cast me in a brilliant play she wrote called *The Beaver Play* (yes, my character fell in love with a beaver in Vermont), and I can always count on an invitation to join her for midnight Mass on Christmas Eve.

I'm so touched that Henriette asked me to write the foreword to this book. I'm not sure I deserve the honor, and I don't think she is completely informed as to how I have made some of my major life decisions. Maybe I'll be the perfect contrast to the highly respected writers whose stories appear within the pages of *No Kidding*.

I knew my limitations at a young age. I was very aware of my inability to multitask by age five. I admitted this to my mother when I came in from playing, spit out my chewing gum, handed it to her, and said, "Mom please hold my gum, I'm going to the bathroom right now, and I can't handle both." The big decisions in my life have always been made in small, significant moments that I can't recover from. These moments are visual, and I play them on a loop in my head.

The profound decision not to have children came out of a thirty-second image I saw on one hot summer day in the early '80s. We were at Jaycee's Dairy in Hanover, Massachusetts. I was home from my sophomore year in college, and my parents couldn't think of anything to do with me except get ice cream. So there I sat, in the backseat of their Volvo eating my usual soft-serve vanilla cone with chocolate jimmies.

Next to us a steaming, overheating, station wagon brimming with young children—four to be exact—pulled up. The oldest one couldn't have been more than five-years-old with his beet-red, sobbing face pressed against the window. They all looked like they had been bathing in Orange Fanta and crying for days. I don't think I would have paid any attention to the driver, except that I recognized her hair. No one had shiny platinum hair like that—except Lila Beck.

Lila Beck was three grades above me in school. I was obsessed with her. She was unlike anybody else in my tiny town. There was nothing about her that was obedient or people-pleasing. She was unflappable. She didn't even seem to mind when somebody called her a slut. She slept with whomever she wanted to sleep with—without any shame. She slept with two best friends. And both guys still liked her. Do you know how hard that is to pull off in a small town?

On the treacherous, bumpy, forty-five minute bus ride to school, while we were supposed to stay seated, Lila would stand at the back of the bus in the aisle wearing her turquoise shorts, defying gravity. She somehow managed to write notes to boys on hot pink paper, apply makeup, and do "walk the dog" with a light-up yoyo, all without holding on. She was a multitasker before the phrase was coined. To someone like me who couldn't crap and chew gum at the same time—she was a white angel.

I was always trying to convince myself that life in New England suburbia wasn't depressing. The houses were pretty, and I had a horse.

But Lila Beck had a huge advantage. Lila Beck had Lila Beck. She seemed complete at fourteen, which to me seemed like such an impossible feat. Lila wasn't a cheerleader, or even a good student. In fact, I read a letter she wrote to my brother that sounded as if it was written by Lenny from *Of Mice and Men*.

I remember the day I knocked on Lila's front door selling Girl Scout cookies. She answered and said she was on the phone. She led me to the kitchen, climbed up onto the counter, sat cross-legged in her bare feet, painted her toe nails white, and blatantly ignored me while she chatted with a friend. I stood there in her kitchen, holding onto my cookie order form, mesmerized. I didn't know what she was, except that she was a different animal, and I couldn't get enough. She could have been President of the United States or the Queen of Monaco. No matter who she was, her life was better than mine. Better than anybody's. I hated the fact that she knew I played the clarinet.

The Girl Scout cookie visit took place when I was eleven or twelve. Eight years later, I'm in the back seat of that Volvo, and I'm seeing Lila Beck for the first time since high school. She didn't look any less pretty. She just looked different. I can't tell you all the thoughts that entered my mind, but I know what the feeling was. The beautiful Lila Beck, the free-spirited rebel that did whatever she wanted whenever she felt like it, was gone. Now she was trapped in a cage of responsibility.

At that moment, my fascination with Lila Beck ended. I didn't want the car or the kids. I didn't want the responsibility or the vulnerability of it all. My only wish in that moment was to be barren.

I'm aware that I could just as easily have been sitting in my parents' car on a different summer day. On a day that was less hot, Lila could have driven up in her shiny car with her handsome husband and her four non-sticky, angelic kids. Then maybe I would have made the decision to have as many kids as my ovaries would allow, but that's not the way it happened. In retrospect, this probably was my most honest moment of knowing my limitations—knowing that I didn't want the selflessness of motherhood.

I don't know whatever happened to Lila Beck. I have no idea how her life turned out, but Lila, if you are reading this now, "Remember me? You've inspired me in ways you can't imagine. You truly did. You made me who I am. Thanks for taking one for the team. I hope it was easier than it looked."

In *No Kidding*, Henriette has cherry-picked some of the best women writers around who have consciously or unconsciously made the decision to not have children. This collection of stories couldn't be more interesting or diverse, and you certainly don't have to be childless, or "child-free" to be moved by them. Some made me laugh out loud, while others made me sob uncontrollably. Whether lighthearted or heartbreaking, they are all unique perspectives on a sometimes delicate topic.

It's clear to me that kids are not in my future. My childbearing years are gone, and to some this fact would be disconcerting. Instead, I take comfort in the camaraderie I share with these cool women who face the same reality.

Jennifer Coolidge
January 2013

Introduction

HENRIETTE MANTEL: "I went to a psychic today, and she told me I'm never going to have children but that I'll have a lifelong companion."

LAURA KIGHTLINGER: "Did she tell you that your companion is going to eat out of a bowl on the floor?"

Years ago, I remember watching *The Tonight Show* with Joan Rivers, who was the guest host. Gloria Steinem, who was about forty years old at the time, was her guest. In her usual obnoxious way, Joan said to Gloria, "You know, my daughter has been the biggest joy in my life and I can't imagine not having her. Don't you regret not having children?" Gloria Steinem didn't miss a beat. She answered, "Well, Joan, if every woman had a child there wouldn't be anybody here to tell you what it's like not to have one." Joan looked at her like that thought had honestly never crossed her mind.

It was a true gift for me to be able to pull together writers who are here to tell you "what it's like not to have one." They share their personal experiences about their lives without giving birth. Whether it is monetary or health issues, courage, apathy, or just plain unadulterated choice that brings these women together, their stories of not having kids made me realize not only am I not alone, but my company is pretty darn great.

Something I learned from pulling this book together (besides the fact that writers are probably the most stubborn people in the world) is that women without children absolutely don't hate the little buggers (okay, maybe Suzy Soro does). Most of them are extremely proud of their relationships with their nieces, nephews, godchildren, neighbors' kids, students, etc., etc., etc. Margaret Mead suggested that the generative impulse could be expressed in other ways, such as passing ideas on to the younger generation through teaching, writing, or by inspiring example. And God knows Hillary Clinton taught us "It Takes a Village" to raise the kids of the world. I feel like these writers are letting all the daughters of the world know it's okay to not have kids. In this day and age, it's so easy to have a kid. Surrogate moms, fertilization treatments, baby-mamas, and wonderful adoption opportunities . . . why not time-share? The traditional rules for having children are long gone. The field is wide open. Some days I feel like the harder choice is to *not* have a kid. But that's probably just me.

To this day, my ninety-one-year-old mom always says about my cousin Shirley, "You know, she never had children." She might as well be saying, "You know, your cousin Shirley lives in a cave in Uruguay and eats bugs, but at least she is happily married." When I decided to ask her what she thought of my not wanting or having kids, she replied, "Well, you certainly have freedom to do whatever you want." And with that conversation, I started contacting my friends about this book.

EVERY TIME MY HUSBAND AND I SEE OUR OLDER RELATIVES THEY ALWAYS ASK, "WHEN ARE YOU GOING TO HAVE KIDS?" IT'S SUCH AN ASSUMPTION THAT YOU SHOULD HAVE KIDS. THAT'S LIKE ME LOOKING AT THEM AND SAYING, "WHEN ARE YOU GOING TO BREAK YOUR HIP?"
—SUE KOLINSKY

I hope you like our book. Thanks for getting this far.

The Morning Dance

Henriette Mantel

"Whatever happens, happens." That's the way I've always felt about having kids. I guess some people would call it ambivalence—I prefer saying I am in Zen with the universe. Whatever cards are dealt, I deal with the feelings when the time comes. I have pushed a lot of things in my life, but I never pushed having children. Partly because I could never imagine raising a child alone and partly because my choices in men have always been just this side of serial killers. But most of all, I never had that gotta-have-a-baby visceral craving that ruled so many of my friends. I like kids. I LOVE kids. I love my nieces and my lone nephew more than life itself. My godchildren make me smile every time I speak their names. My reason for not having kids wasn't that I hate the little buggers, it was that I've always felt fate will let me know if I'm supposed to be a mom or not. Fate never brought me a man I would love to get pregnant with, fate never called me to raise a child alone, and fate never knocked me up, so here I am, childless. And that's exactly where I was when I met Jimmy. He had an eleven-year-old daughter, and my first thought was, "This could be fun. I wouldn't mind joining a show like this in the second act."

The first time I met Lil was on Father's Day. Not too much holiday pressure to meet the offspring of the man you had only been dating for four months, right? I got to their apartment on that beautiful spring day, and it was all I could do to ring the bell. I felt like I was meeting the Last Emperor when really I was meeting an eleven-year-old daughter of a guy I was nuts about. Jimmy opened the door and there she was, standing with him and smiling, wearing a blue T-shirt and lavender leggings, her face half hidden by a mess of hair, which looked like she'd made an attempt at brushing but somewhere along the line gave up. I could tell she wanted to hug me, but what I got was a very polite, held-in handshake. She was as cute as a button. She was so checking me out as we walked to the restaurant. I was checking her out too. You never know if these monsters are going to be friend or foe. I was hoping for the best and was pretty sure it would be fine since I could feel we were both trying to hold in our glee. Now that I look back, we should have just started dancing right there on the spot. But we didn't. After all, I was meeting my boyfriend's daughter. I was *supposed* to be an adult.

We went to a restaurant that Jimmy chose. He is vegan right down to his sneakers, though the place had meat on the menu, so I guess he was thinking of us too. Totally vegan is just a bit over the top for my dietary beliefs. In fact, those people might be nuts. Come on, no eggs? But it was certainly good for a conversation starter since I told Lil I grew up raising chickens. She was intrigued and asked me if I had a problem eating them. "I hate them alive and enjoy them dead," was all I could come up with. She laughed with a certain mischievous disbelief but then asked me if I could tell the difference between fresh eggs and eggs that had been in the store awhile. Loving her intrigue I said, "The only true way to know if they are fresh is to squeeze them out of the chicken yourself." "Oh my gosh," her curiosity rising, "did you really do that?" "No, but once my mom needed eggs for a cake and my Dad did." She laughed and said she would like to follow an egg from the time it leaves the chicken all the way to her dish.

Throughout the meal, Lil bubbled over with conversation. "Dad said you had a horse when you were growing up. That is my *dream!*" We went on to talk about everything from horses to clothes to haircuts and acting. I'm pretty sure we both fell in love that day. Or at least I did. It was the most connected I had felt in a conversation in a long time.

The house I grew up in in Vermont has always been somewhat of a holy ground to me. My best friend calls it Tara. It's a big deal if I take someone there. One weekend, Jimmy, Lil, and I headed to Vermont to hang out. Lil was a bit stressed since she had to memorize her scenes to play Helena in a performance of *A Midsummer Night's Dream* at her Shakespeare camp. We practiced together, and she was great. I wasn't a bad Demetrius either. She said, "I have found Demetrius like a jewel, mine own, and not mine own," and it rolled off her tongue like she was talking about her favorite dessert.

We laughed about all the thous and thees and thines. She asked why they talked like that, and I answered, "You'll have to study that in college; I have no idea." She then said what I later learned was a pretty regular response to many questions: "My mother might know." Through those "My mother might know" responses, I came to love her mom too. But every time Lil mentioned her, I could feel the pain of divorce oozing out of her pores. In fact, she made me feel I wanted her parents to get back together and live happily ever after just so I could relieve her eleven-year-old hurt. Is this what it's like to have a kid? You don't want them to feel any pain? When it comes to the kids in my life, I always think of Bruce Springsteen's song where he says, "If I had one wish, in this godforsaken world, kids, that your mistakes would be your own, that your sins would be your own." But with Lil, it felt like she suffered the mistakes of her parents, not herself. I had such empathy for this kid I was starting to adore.

I wanted Lil to have good memories of her childhood. But that's what most parents want, right? So off we went into the woods in my family's all-terrain vehicle. Lil was a total nature kid, at least in the book sense. She loved wildlife and, thanks to her Dad, had quite a bit of knowledge about endangered species. So darn if she didn't spot a turtle right by our path. We stopped and stared for what felt like forever before we decided to take it up to the house to show everybody. Me picking him up with my bare hands made Lil scream, but she was smiling from ear to ear when we arrived back at the house and showed him off. My sister immediately found some nail polish so Lil could put her initials on our new turtle friend's shell. I had been painting turtles since I was a kid, so I was glad Lil was into it too. She looked at Jimmy to get approval for such a savage act of joy. He looked perplexed, evidently conflicted because he was trying to figure out where nail polish on turtles fit into his environmental concerns. "Okay, just do it," he finally surrendered with a big smile. Lil painted her bright red initials carefully, right across that turtle's back. We took some pictures, bid farewell, and set Turtle-Guy free to find his friends and family. We hoped the humiliation of a makeover wouldn't be too much for him to bear. Lil reminded us that manicures do wear off, which seemed to calm Jimmy's nerves considerably.

Back in the city a few weeks later, Lil and I were doing one of our favorite things: walking Pip, their reality-escaping beagle. She said, "I picked you." "Who? What? Where?" I said. She giggled and repeated, "I picked you." Maybe she could see I wasn't sure what she was talking about. "Dad was dating three women, and I picked you." I answered, "Gee, that is such a nice compliment. Thanks." "Yeah, he was dating a general from the Army [wow, what competition] and another lady with a stupid name [relieved the name "Henriette" isn't stupid] so I picked you." How was I supposed to say anything to answer this sweet, naive, kind, and interested eleven-year-old? We kept yakety-yakking while I went a little nuts because Jimmy had told me I was the only one he was dating, and who was I not to believe him? Right? Oh no, was this another bad-choice boyfriend? And if so, whose feelings do I consider first? Lil's? Mine? Jimmy's? Why the hell was Jimmy sharing the details of his love life with his eleven-year-old daughter anyway? God, was this his fatherly way? To talk to his daughter about his love life? Yuck. I thought of my friend Jill's divorce agreement where she and her ex couldn't even introduce their kids to their respective love interests until they were in the picture for a year. Or my friend Sheila, who told me that the thing that screwed her up the most in life was the revolving door of girlfriends her Dad had while she was growing up. Wait a sec, I'm not her mom, I have no say in what her Dad tells her and how. But what's my role as an adult in this relationship? Was I a step-girlfriend? Is this the kind of crap married parents argue about? Who decides how and what information to give a kid? Good God, this wasn't even my kid; why was I getting so freaked out? I felt like I was falling in love with Lil and starting to look at her father in a very different way, especially if this eleven-year-old's perceptions were on the mark.

Now are you starting to see why I've never wanted kids? My choice in beaus has always blown chunks, to put it nicely. Could this be another one of those choices?

Toward the end of the summer, I went to Los Angeles to work for a week. I got home on the red-eye and was absolutely exhausted. I woke up at 11:00 AM to a text from Jimmy. Only it was Lil. "Are you home? It's Lil!! Dad and I want to know if you can come over!!!" I texted back that I was really tired but yeah, I'd love to come over in the afternoon. "Yippeeeeeeeeeeeeeee," she sent. Her favorite thing to say was "Yippee," and I have to say I just don't hear that word enough. I hadn't seen either Lil or the man I truly missed for ten days. When I got off the subway, Lil came *running* toward me, in a sweet skirt and top that matched. She had her long light brown hair in braids and a huge smile on her face. She hugged me and said, "I missed you and I LOVE your pants." I answered, "I missed you and I love your skirt." Jimmy came a little more slowly with Pip and hugged me too. I could feel something was off. Maybe he was just tired. Or maybe I was tired, or we were both tired. He said he was glad our pack was back intact.

When I was growing up, my friend Susan always had a boyfriend. By the time we were thirty, she had already been divorced twice with one kid from each marriage. Along the way, I was always a loyal friend and defended her choices in men to my mom, who would say, "She's in love with love, not him." I started to wonder if I was in love with being part of a family unit and that it didn't really matter who was in it. Wait, I knew I loved Lil. But as for her father . . .

We got back to their apartment, and I realized how exhausted I was from my trip. After dinner Lil wanted to watch a movie, but I could barely keep my eyes open. They both agreed it was okay if I retired early.

Call me old-fashioned, but I had not yet gotten over the nervousness of sleeping over with Jimmy when Lil was there, so I had packed my cutest summer pajamas to let her know it was all about fun. I was brushing my teeth, and sure enough Lil came in and said, "I love those pajamas. They are so happy. I'd like to get my mom some just like that." Scared to tell her they were half price at Victoria's Secret (probably the least sexy thing in the catalog) I said, "Oh, next time I go by the place where I got them I'll see if they have some for your mom." She was absolutely delighted especially, I think, that I mentioned her mom with love. She didn't seem used to her mom being a positive character around her Dad's house. But I had nothing against her mom. In fact, I kinda liked her mom. Sometimes Jimmy would say something about her mom in disgust and resentment, and when I would just hit the mute button instead of confirming his opinion, I realized how much resentment there was, at least from his side. Lil had to have felt it too.

I woke up in the morning to find Jimmy and Lil already out in the kitchen. Lil was talking a blue streak, and Jimmy was trying to make her some breakfast. Lil came over and gave me a hug, "Good morning." Jimmy handed me a cup of coffee. Then he went to the living room with his laptop and started reading whatever it was he read every morning for hours. It didn't occur to me then, but now I realize he was probably finding out what the "other woman" was up to. Something was sure going on with this guy, and if he wasn't going to tell me, I was just going to go along in my happy way till the dam broke—and I could feel it starting to give. Other times in my life I had pushed too hard, too soon with men about issues they didn't want to talk about. So he was reaping the benefits of the other bongo-brains I had dated and would not get pushed by me. At least not yet.

So for our Sunday morning time, Jimmy was in the chair and Lil and I were on the sofa joking around while we tried in the usual futile way to get Pip to roll over. "Roll over," we would both say through our giggling, and we'd put a treat on the other side of him. Poor Pip seemed confused, but the excitement we both had at even the thought of Pip actually doing some tricks overrode all order. Lil literally pushed Pip to roll over and then gave him the snack with a loud, "Yippee Pippy!" Neither one of us could stop laughing.

Pip just wasn't cooperating with his two crazy trainers, so I jokingly suggested maybe we should turn him in for a new model. All of the sudden Jimmy raised his voice and said, "Don't talk to my daughter like that!" I looked at him in shock. Lil snapped to my defense, "Dad *lighten up . . .*" We both laughed kind of nervously, so to break the tension, I grabbed Lil to tickle her and teased, "I was only kidding, I was only kidding, I love Pip, I love you . . ." With that Jimmy got up and announced he was taking Pip out for a walk. Lil looked at me like, "Oooh-KAY!"

After he was gone, Lil said, "I'm sorry my Dad is so grouchy. He's always that way in the morning." "Oh my gosh Lil, you don't ever have to apologize for him; it's okay if he is in a grouchy mood; we all are sometimes." She was obviously relieved that I didn't hold it against her. The look on her face made me wonder what the hell Jimmy had put his eleven-year-old through. I started to think about when I was that age, about how I would try to cover up for my mom's depressed/angry behavior. Even though it hurt me, as long as I apologized to the outside world, life would be fine. So Lil had turned into me. I had turned into my dad, who was always overcompensating for Mom's behavior and trying to just let my eleven-year-old butt have fun, and, gee, guess who Jimmy was? He was my depressed and angry mom. At least that was the way it was when I was eleven. Now my mom will be the first one to tell you that bringing up kids was the joy of her life. I wish she had told me then. But instead back then, my brother and I would make each other laugh, and suddenly it was all forgotten. Lil didn't have a brother, but she did have me, and I wasn't about to let this kid feel like

I was anything but positive. One time I asked a friend of mine who is an only child why she and her wonderful only-child husband didn't want kids. She answered, "We decided to stop the madness and put an end to the tragedy that would be called 'family.'" All I could reply to her was, "Boy, I feel ya on that one."

Breaking my reverie (and I was deep into it) Lil said, "Hey, let's do the morning dance before Dad gets back." I had taught Lil this silly "morning dance" that I had made up about forty years before to irritate my brother. What you do is sing, "Good morning, good morning, it's a beautiful morning!" while dancing wildly in any way you feel with total delight just waffling through you. Of course I took her up on the offer, and we both did the morning dance with reckless abandon. We flopped on the couch in exhaustion, laughing, when Jimmy walked back in. He went straight to the kitchen.

Lil grabbed a book just like I had at that age when I felt tension in the house. I went to the kitchen to refill my coffee and give Jimmy a kiss on the neck. "Wow, you smell like cigarettes," I said. "Yeah, I started smoking while you were gone. I've had some drinks too," he replied. I had no idea what to say. I retreated to the living room with a chill through my heart. Early on in the relationship, I had broken up with him because I saw the addiction issues. But like a good addict, he had calmed my nerves and told me he was quitting everything. And I honestly believe he did. Until he didn't.

The next weekend, Jimmy and I started breaking up. A few days later, with a flurry of late-night phone calls and 5:00 AM emails, it was over.

Letting go of a boyfriend is one thing. Letting ago of an eleven-year-old is a whole other thing. I was haunted by the fact that this sensitive kid I had come to love might feel abandoned or betrayed by me.

My requests to see or write Lil were unanswered by Jimmy. He had made up his mind, and I was out. Therefore, Lil was out of my life too.

I was devastated by the breakup. But who was I more in love with? Jimmy or Lil? Since I'm all about charts and graphs, I tend to look to the five stages of death when a relationship ends. But how could I possibly put Lil in the death category? And what was I supposed to do about her? Was there anything I *could* do? I knew in my heart there would soon be relief that Jimmy and I had broken up, but I had never experienced anything like letting go of Lil, so relief seemed impossible to foresee.

I confided in my divorced friend Laura, who has two girls and went through a breakup with a guy her kids were very attached to, when it occurred to me that I wanted to call Lil's mom. I was scared, but I couldn't take the weight anymore, and I had to take action. I walked over to Central Park, sat on a quiet bench, and made the call. "Hi, uhm, this is Henriette, and I used to date your ex, Jimmy, and uhm, if this is over any boundary for you, you don't have to talk to me, I just really want to say something."

She answered so kindly, "No, please, it's fine, what is it?" "I miss Lil . . ." I burst out crying, and she replied with, "Ahhhhhhhh." I might be mistaken, but I think I heard her voice crack too. I went on to tell her how bad I felt that Jimmy wouldn't let me say good-bye to Lil and I just didn't ever want her to think I abandoned her. "Lil cried for a week after Jimmy told her you broke up," she said. It was all I could do to talk between tears. I am not much of a crier, but you wouldn't have known it that day. I couldn't stop crying. I just felt pain about Lil's pain. And my own pain. I was a blubbering fool talking to a woman I had met once briefly in passing. She handled it well. I didn't.

I walked out of the park still crying and sat on a bench. Even though I was relieved that Lil's mom understood and would let Lil know I was thinking of her, I realized I wasn't just crying for Lil; I was feeling the extreme pain of separation from someone I love. Not an adult that hopefully knows who they are, and figures out ways to mourn or live with the pain of loss, but a kid who loved me in such an innocent way—just as I had loved her. The innocence for me was about loving without thinking of the possibility it would ever end.

I lost my closest brother at a young age. I watched my parents suffer, and, even though they stayed together because they truly loved each other, our family was never the same. I had loved my brother Jeff more than life itself, and though I learned to live with that loss, I still miss him. I didn't know Lil that long, but sometimes one person in your life says one thing and you remember it forever. Maybe it was my age, maybe it was her age, maybe it was just the universe putting my relationship with her in front of me to make me look at the bigger picture of my life that never included having my own children . . . or maybe she was put in front of me so that I would edit a book of essays by women who are living a life without kids. Yeah, that sounds more like the God I know—birth on paper is the perfect godly gift for me. And after it's published, I don't even have to send it to college.

Even though Lil was the child who really got me thinking about why I never had kids, I still don't feel like I missed anything by not having them. With my luck, my kid might be the next Carrie Nation, Gaddafi (I've always been attracted to dark men), or Lindsay Lohan. What would I do with *that*? And yes, there is a *little* sadness around that, but there's also a *little* sadness around the fact I may never get to go to the moon. Jeez, you can't do everything in this lifetime, and having kids isn't even *on* my bucket list . . .

I miss encouraging Lil with her acting career, discussing movies and horses, and walking Pip. She taught me a certain girl-self love I had never felt before. I learned how to love the eleven-year-old girl that I had been with her, just riding horses, pedicuring turtles, and enjoying life. She helped me get in touch with the upside of my childhood, and for that I am forever grateful.

Lil gave me a tiny glimpse into a part of life that I hadn't experienced—motherhood. Even though my cats and dogs call me mom, according to experts it's just not the same. And even though I know some of my sisters' kids (hello, teenagers) and my godchildren some days *wish* I were their mom, that is different too. From Lil I learned how I would rather stick needles in my eyes than ever inflict emotional pain on a child. And most of all, I confirmed once again it's hard to beat the joy I feel when a kid is laughing. But do I *want* or *need* that kid laughing to come out of my own loins? Absolutely not. If there's one thing I learned from Hillary Clinton, it's that I'm part of the village, but I sure don't need to make my own tent full. Invitation accepted.

I'm sure Lil has moved on, like kids do, but she will always have a place in my heart reserved just for her. Someday I will run into her and say, "You were my eleven-year-old sage in a skirt, and just remember, whatever happens, happens—but the morning dance will last forever."

I Wouldn't Know Where to Begin

Margaret Cho

I don't have children, and I am not sure if I have wanted them or never wanted them. It's weird not to be able to decide. Kids are great, and many of my friends now have almost-grown-up kids, like in their late teens and early twenties, and I see these tall beings I once held in my arms, and I am alarmed, amused, and I want to cry, just for the passage of time and how it grows us like plants. I think about how, during all these years they've grown up, I must have grown down. That's awful to realize.

Korean children get a lot of fuss made over them, I guess because life was tough in the old country, and it was a big deal if you survived. There's a big party thrown when you are one hundred days old, followed by another when you make it to one whole year. My parents took a lot of pictures of me at these parties, although I don't remember a thing as I was really drunk at both. From the pictures I see the cake though—all these big multicolored rice cakes, each pastel stripe a steamed layer of pounded and steamed rice flour, not sweet like birthday cake but a delicious treat all the same. It looks like a chewy Neapolitan ice cream, or a gay pride flag made of carbs. It's the best and I want it, but I think wanting that cake isn't enough reason to have a baby.

My mother goes crazy over babies. Some people just do. They love 'em! I never have. Babies scare me more than anything. They're tiny and fragile and impressionable—and someone else's! As much as I hate borrowing stuff, that is how much I hate holding other people's babies. It's too much responsibility. Of course they are lovely and warm and adorable, and it's so funny when they decide they like you and hold you in return, but I am frightened of doing something wrong that will alter them forever. Give them a weird look and they might be talking to their therapist about me fifty years later. My mom has none of this fear. She loves kids to the degree that she will talk to other moms about their kids—she's always done this—even white moms! This was so embarrassing when I was growing up. I was like, "Mom! Shut up! They're WHITE!"

When it comes to children, my mom doesn't believe in borders. She loves all children, and that's a good example of mothering the world. I need to do that, but before I can, I need to get over my fear of kids in the first place.

It might not be a fear of kids themselves, as in truth I usually get along with them pretty well. They like my tattoos and my uncomplicated child/adult face. They identify with my orange shoes. I look like I would let them get away with stuff, and I do. My fear of having children is that, frankly, I just don't want to love anyone that much. I have my own problems with love, and I have processed and played the same games for a lifetime, but what if I had to do that with someone I actually MADE?! (Or went all the way to China and adopted. This is not a joke—I have long thought I would adopt one of those baby girls from China, because really, who's going to know the difference?)

I don't know if I could stand that kind of commitment, or, if I am really honest, I don't think I could handle being that vulnerable to someone else. My child would have my heart completely—having never truly given that over, in all my relationships in my life, starting with myself, I wouldn't even know where to begin.

What to Expect When You're Never Expecting

Bonnie Datt

"Okay, here's the truth, I can't have children," I told my cabdriver somberly. I attempted to look distraught, my lips quivering. And my ploy worked. Finally this man, who'd relentlessly argued that I would change my mind about my decision to not have children, clammed up and began focusing intently on the road. Yes, after years of being told by complete strangers that I didn't know my own mind, I'd finally learned the secret to get people to stop insisting, "You'll eventually want to have kids." I just had to lie about it.

Not having children was a decision I made when I was practically a child myself. In my early teens, I became very sick (not fatally). It turned out I was allergic to almost everything—foods, chemicals, pollens—if it tasted or smelled good, I was allergic to it. It was sort of a girl-in-the-plastic-bubble existence.[1] Managing my health wasn't easy, so I quickly decided I wasn't going to have children. I didn't want to risk passing on my condition. Once I made that decision, I was unwavering in it, but everyone else was skeptical. They were sure I'd change my mind.

When I was growing up, it wasn't an issue. Most teenage girls didn't want to be parents, since back then, single motherhood had yet to become a gateway to MTV stardom. And frankly, even if one of my female classmates had wanted to get pregnant, I doubt she could have, since most weren't having sex—with the probable exception of Jessica, the only girl in gym class whose underwear didn't look like it had been bought by her mother. I'm pretty sure my "no sex" theory was correct, since most of the guys my friends dated in high school now have spouses named "Jake" or "Heath." While not many of my schoolmates had mustaches, it turns out that there were a lot of beards.

In my early twenties, the child issue never came up, because I was now a stand-up comic, and all the men I dated were stand-up comics. The only children most of them were willing to share attention with were their own narcissistic inner ones. But when I moved to New York, stopped doing stand-up, and began dating "grown-ups" with "real jobs," that all changed. Much to my shock, many of the men I dated refused to believe I didn't want children.

There was Jack, a thirty-year-old prosecuting attorney. It was our second date, and we were having Chinese take-out in my miniscule studio, an apartment so small we had to studiously ignore my bed that sat just inches away from the table.

Possibly due to the bed's proximity, the issue of children came up. I casually mentioned I didn't want any.

"Come on," he gasped incredulously. "Really? Never?"

"Never," I countered, starting to wish I'd directed all his attention to the bed. Then we'd be too busy to be having this conversation.

Jack grilled me as though I was one of his hostile witnesses. "So let me get this straight," he repeated for what seemed like the fifty-third time, but what in reality was probably only the fifty-second. "You don't think you'll ever change your mind? There is no possibility of that EVER happening?"

Exhausted, I weakened. "Well, I guess it's theoretically possible that someday I might change my mind, but—"

"—See? I knew you wanted to have kids!" Jack crowed victoriously and then happily dug into his kung pao chicken. Case closed.

Jack never explained why he refused to believe I didn't want kids. Perhaps, like many people, he assumed that if you had estrogen coursing through your body, you would naturally want to own a BabyBjörn.

Then there was Steve. He worked in publishing, and although he was only in his early twenties, he had all the stages of his life conventionally mapped out. He assumed I did too. We'd been dating for about a month when I told him how I felt about kids, but like Jack, he refused to believe me. But at least he gave a reason.

"You'll change your mind," he insisted. "You'll need someone to take care of you when you're old."

I was appalled by Steve's attitude. Even though I didn't want children, I was sure that if I were the kind of person who did, it wouldn't be for such a mercenary reason. Steve and I didn't last too long.

After the Jack and Steve incidents, I figured I should keep my mouth shut about not wanting kids—at least on early dates. It seemed like most guys really wanted to have children.

But then, along came Chris, a cute, brilliant, funny, British, Cambridge-educated banker.[2] I liked him immediately, but I feared that, as a corporate type, he and his views might be too traditional for me.

Chris and I were on our first date, at a small restaurant in the East Village. It was one of those amazing first dates, where you eat and you talk and the evening just whizzes by. Everything was going really well, until a baby at a nearby table started crying. Without thinking, I grimaced. Chris, being a cute, brilliant, funny, British Cambridge-educated banker, immediately honed in on its meaning.[3]

"You don't like children?" he queried.

Damn that baby for making me lose my game!

"Um, no, not really," I said sweetly and shrugged, trying to stem off the awful discussion I was sure would follow.

But all Chris responded with was, "Really?" and he said it in the thrilled tone a man might use if his date had just said, "I love giving blow jobs!"

I probed cautiously, "You don't want kids?"

"Nooo!" he responded, emphatically.

"Really?" I questioned, in the thrilled tone a woman might use if her date had just said, "I don't like receiving blow jobs."

We smiled across the table, as imaginary slot machines jangled winning jackpots in our heads. *Kaching! Kaching! Kaching!*

Chris and I eventually married—a happy, fulfilling, and child-free relationship.

Knowing about my health, my loving parents never pushed to be grandparents. "Having children isn't for everyone," Mom explained wisely. She was kind enough not to add, "It can be tough. You were a challenge."

My British mother-in-law, with her innate kindness and impeccable manners, wasn't a problem either. And our friends all supported our decision. Some became particularly emphatic in their support while diapering their own screaming babies.

Despite all this backing, once I was married, I ran across even more people who refused to believe I didn't want children. This came primarily from inquisitive strangers I'd been arbitrarily forced to spend long periods of time with, like cab drivers and seatmates on planes and trains. Their inquisitions all followed the same pattern.

"Are you married?"

"Yes."

Then the inevitable, "Kids?"

"No."

"Gonna have them?"

"Nope."

Which should have been the end of that. But it never was.

"Oh, you'll have kids. You're young; you'll change your mind."

It went on and on. Every single one of them was sure they knew me better than I knew myself. Much like pregnant women's stomachs, which strangers feel they have a right to touch, these people felt that my fertility was their business.

I should have just told them to butt out, but I was raised in the Midwest, so this rude option never crossed my mind. Thus was born my all-purpose taxicab "confession."

Even though I had no idea whether I was fertile or not, I began saying, "I can't have children," to anyone who would belabor my lack of wanting to be in labor. I even perfected a small, yet dramatic, sniffle.

Sure, I felt a tad guilty making strangers feel bad, but I justified it by the fact that I was only responding to people who were nagging me about something that was none of their business. Did I tell my airplane seatmate she'd regret having six children—and would eventually put five up for adoption? No, I did not! So who were they to tell me I didn't know my own mind?

Look, it's not that I hate kids. I have three amazing teenage godchildren and an adorable toddler-aged niece—all of whom I'm crazy about. And occasionally, as I've helped dress a Barbie doll, or read aloud from *Curious George,* or watched one of them graduate with honors from high school, I've felt a surge or two of maternal yearnings. But then a toy breaks, a diaper is soiled, or a fight breaks out over an "unfair" curfew, and those feelings quickly disperse.

Will I ever regret my decision not to have children? Who knows? Having seen my parents' health decline dramatically as they aged, and having had to take responsibility for my father, I did recently start to wonder, who would look after Chris and me if we get old and infirm?

And then it hit me: If that day comes, I will track down all my old cab drivers, plane and train seatmates, Jack, and of course that mercenary, Steve. I will write them all letters telling them they were right—right to choose to have their own children. Then I'll add that I've just broken my hip, and ask them to please send over one of their kids to help me in the bathroom.

No BabyBjörns for me. My body, my choice.

All of It

Nora Dunn

The women I know who have children never say they want another person. They always say they want another baby. They don't seem to realize that no matter how many babies they have, the baby will always get bigger. Their baby's fat will dissolve, and they will start to walk and talk, and eventually their baby will tell them to go to hell. They don't see that having babies might mean they become such a terrible parent they have to appear with their husbands on the Dr. Phil show. I have an acquaintance who sang to me the praises of adoption only to have one of her adopted daughters falsely accuse her of abuse. Still, women who have had babies long to have another baby, to fall in love with another innocent who needs them above all else in the world, and who smells like a brand-new car. Cradling a baby is addictive, and even I am not immune to the power of it.

I have cradled other people's babies and considered kidnapping them. But I've never done it. I've never tried to steal or buy a baby. I have taken credit for other people's babies while in my charge, accepting compliments about how beautiful they are with grace and humility and then, after returning them, I have felt barren. What am I to call myself, a baroness?

I have fantasized about finding a baby on a bike trail and taking it home, not to the place where I actually live, but a house with a yard and dog and an income that allows for private schools and college. In that house there's a handsome husband who is tall with very nice arms but beyond that has no distinguishable characteristics.

Women without children don't really know what we're missing, though we feel at times that we missed out or missed the boat. We missed the boat because we were too busy being childless. No one but a childless woman can understand how much work it takes not to have a child and how off-putting it is to particularly smug women who have children and a career and a husband and an endless series of private Pilates. We don't have a badge of honor to pull out of our diaper sacks. At the cocktail party where we're asked if we have children, we must answer, "No." And then put a winsome expression on our face as if to say we know how tragic that is. We might mention a miscarriage or two, but certainly never blurt out the "A" word.

In the current abortion debate, there is no talk of children. Those who are anti-abortion never mention them. They seem to be the same people who want to cut food stamps and get rid of social programs that might help children and mothers. They never talk about nineteen–year-old fetuses. They don't talk of war or hunger or about how much it costs to buy shoes and socks and how hard it must be to have children without a washer and dryer. They never seem to take into account who the father is, or who the boyfriends might be. I never wanted to have a baby if I wasn't positive I could give it a wonderful life and my undivided attention. I didn't get that from my own mother. When I was little, I didn't understand that there is no such thing as undivided attention. My feeling was I needed to become a good mother to myself before I invented a child that needed one.

I have amazing friends who share their amazing children and who think I'm amazing because I have patience with them. Well, patience is easy when you know it doesn't have to last that long. I like children. I like spending time with them and listening to them. I like making things with them out of paper and clay. But eventually they wander off and become infatuated with people their own age, and I find myself seeking another seven-year-old to relate to. I like children, but I never longed for the birth part where they tear apart your vagina while some guy you slept with is gawking at you with a camcorder. I decided long before I didn't have children that the father would never be allowed in the birthing room. He would be at work.

One of my dearest friends says that being a mother means making it up as you go along. She's a great mother, but her life has not been perfect. She never claimed to have it all and tells funny and disastrous stories about her experiences with her first baby girl. I do the same. I tell funny and disastrous stories about my own improvised life. My friends with children are no different from my friends who don't have them. Almost. Neither group brags endlessly about their gifted child. They talk about other things. And if I do find myself in a room full of obnoxious parents and their precocious brainchildren, I leave. Just like that. I don't have to collect my own children or backpacks. I don't have to engage in endless small talk at the door as I leave a playdate. In my world, a playdate is something quite different. It's not rated PG.

I have only once longed for motherhood. I had witnessed a petty crime, a young man breaking into a car. I called the police who arrived after he and his female accomplice left the scene. Later, I was asked to identify the suspects. I felt sorry for the guy as he stepped out of the police car for me to see him, but when the girl stepped out, my heart broke. She was young but looked old. She was scrawny and uncared-for. She looked at me with sad and weary eyes. Even her rage had been extinguished. I became so overwhelmed with maternal instinct I wanted to cradle her in my arms and restore the innocence she had lost, and all of her baby fat. I wanted to apologize to her for being such a rotten mother.

Later at lunch in a restaurant, as I sat over a bowl of brown rice and tofu, I thought of that girl and felt terrible that I had never taken her shopping, had never made sure she got to her soccer game or finished her homework, and had never taught her the joys of becoming a powerful and self-sufficient woman. I thought of finding her and making up for all of her losses. Suddenly, not being a mother became one of my regrets, and the tears that dropped into my rice bowl gave the dish its only flavor.

Nobody has it all. Among my regrets will always be that I never raised a girl to womanhood. But the sadness of that afternoon wore off, and my life became once again what it is: a collection of achievements and failures, great expectations and disappointments, loves and losses, and nieces and nephews whom I adore and who seem to like me too. I don't know motherhood, but it seems to know me. I'm proud of myself. My inner child is an honor student.

The Greatest Thing I Never Did

Julie Halston

T he only doll I had even a remote interest in was Chatty Cathy. I took sadistic pleasure in pulling the string on her back and hearing what she had to say. But after the same ten phrases, I realized Chatty Cathy wasn't chatty, she was autistic.

All my dolls ended up neglected in the garage or, worse, heads-down in the garbage. My younger sister rescued many of my dolls so my family didn't have to go through the shame of Doll Family Court. As an adolescent, I was neither tomboy nor girly-girl. I was gender fluid before the term existed. I'd like to think I was ahead of my time, but maybe I was just weird. In high school I once wrote that my ambition in life was "to not get pregnant." I thought it was a funny, but no one laughed. I was sent for counseling.

Now before you think my pathology might make me a candidate for the Manson family, just know my disdain for dolls did not extend to animals, plant life, or babies. I was properly respectful of all and even became a much sought-after babysitter. I just never wanted to make it a permanent deal.

This noninterest in children continued into adulthood, so I just assumed I had a narcissistic personality disorder, but my shrink assured me I wasn't successful enough for that yet. Thank you.

But as every comic performer knows, timing is everything, and my timing for kids always seemed to be off. I was never quite ready. "Ready" in my mind meant the right guy, a secure career, and maybe even a deep, abiding love of children brought on by the tug of maternal instinct. Some of my friends who never before expressed interest in children told me they suddenly felt "baby pangs"—stirrings that made them want to nurture a baby deep within their wombs. I suggested it might be gas.

But as my shrink nicely reminded me, I've been known to make mistakes; could I even entertain the notion of motherhood?

"You're a modern gal," he said, "forget the guy, have a kid on your own; lots of women are doing it."

So . . .

I went to a meeting of Single Mothers By Choice. I met many single mothers by choice, and I am here to tell you they were NOT single by choice.

OHMYGOD!

I fled.

And got a new shrink.

It was after that Single Mothers meeting I realized the only thing that interests me in having a child is picking the name. I LOVE naming things, whether a cat, a story, or a child. So I got two cats (Gypsy and

Harvey), wrote a bad story with a great title ("The House that Loss Built"), and suggested names to pregnant friends. A few choices were even seriously considered. I was thrilled.

My soul faced the truth. I didn't want the love and responsibility of a child. I wanted the love and responsibility of a coterie of gay men and sassy women. Or sassy men and gay women. Either way kids weren't in the equation, but cocktails + smart talk = happiness. I put my eggs on hold and rode the career train. And as they say in biblical parlance:

"And lo and behold, she became a minor cult figure and it was good."

"And the minor cult figure even married and all was right in the Land."

Now coupled, thin with a prewar co-op, I came into my mid-forties with the breathtaking confidence that can only come with the most delusional. And then what has now become known as "that weekend" happened. I had a pregnancy scare. I was late and feeling very nauseous every morning with extremely tender breasts. *How could this be, I can't be pregnant, I'm too old to be pregnant, right? RIGHT???* Well the short answer of course is that I could be pregnant.

In my mother's time, this would be called a "Change-of-Life" Baby or even a "Change-of-Heart" Baby. In my time this is called:

HOW THE FUCK DID THIS HAPPEN?

My husband and I were both startled yet maybe—dare we say maybe—a little, a tad, a scooch excited by the prospect. My hormones were crazy; I couldn't keep a thought in my head. I began to understand how pregnant women and new moms can go completely insane and end up on the cover of *The New York Post*. I shelled out the bucks for the home pregnancy test but was such a bundle of nerves I couldn't properly urinate on the stick. My husband was less panicked, and I even noticed a bit of a strut in his walk. This weekend was now taking on primal, anthropological properties.

Would the baby be healthy? Would I be healthy? What about money?

How do we pay for college? Shit, we're New Yorkers: How do we pay for kindergarten?

And for God's sake what do we name it?! Of course I went into high gear. A girl will be Grace Gardner Howard, a.k.a. Gigi Howard, and she will be a TV reporter; and if a boy, Benjamin Gardner Howard, a.k.a. Ben Howard, and he will write fiction.

Oy vey.

Two days later, my doctor told me not only was I not pregnant, I was starting menopause. Menopause.

Well that gave me pause.

I was sad about not being pregnant . . . for about an hour. And then honestly I was relieved. Really relieved.

I was not relieved however about being middle-aged. I felt . . . what's the right adjective? Horrible.

Getting older isn't all dreadful, but it does mean your field of vision isn't endless. Life becomes about fewer options, not more. I became rather reflective after "that weekend." Socrates said it: *"Know Thyself."* "That guy was on to something. I may not understand a lot of things, like math or Ryan Seacrest's popularity, but one thing was certain to me—I was not meant to be a mother. It was the greatest thing I never did.

Two months later, I opened the door to the Shubert Theater to begin rehearsals with director Sam Mendes and legendary star Bernadette Peters. Irony of ironies, I was cast as one of the strippers in the iconic Broadway musical *Gypsy*. Great show, great title, and all about a mother who shouldn't have been one.

On Not Choosing Children

Janette Barber

Not having children is my biggest regret, and if I had it all to do over again, I would do exactly the same thing. I always knew I would regret it. Between my first and second years of college, I had a summer job at Barker's Department Store. There was a woman there named Berta who worked along with me in the fitting room for the women's clothing section. I can see her in my head to this day. She was probably in her late fifties, about the same age I am now. Tallish, stocky build, short brown hair streaked with gray. She was very nice but had a pervasive sadness about her. One night Berta told me she and her husband—they'd been together almost forty years—had decided when they got married to not have children. Neither had wanted children; they'd wanted to be able to travel and be free to live their lives. To her dismay, now that she was older, she felt it had been the mistake of her life not to have had a child. She'd spend time with her nieces and nephews and then go home and mourn the children she did not have. When she told me that story, way back there when I was eighteen, I thought to myself, "That will be me."

My father used to say, "Having kids is death. It's death." That's a direct quote. He said it a lot. He was a divorced single parent whose own mother had died when he was eleven and who was sad every day of his life. As it turns out, "Having kids is death" is kind of catchy. It sticks in your head. Live the life you dream, or have kids and die.

Throughout my life I thought a lot about having kids. Once I even floated the idea to my sister to see if she was interested, since I simply could not comprehend, even in fantasy, that I would ever be in a lasting relationship with a man. In my twenties I once told my father that, as opposed to it as he was, there was a slight chance I might want to have children. The reason, I said, was because I was the youngest and likely to be the last of the three of us to die. He stopped in his tracks to turn and face me and said, "You're right. Who will bury you?" That remains a concern.

When I was a kid, the idea of accidentally getting pregnant was terrifying to me. When I was ten or eleven, I became so concerned I decided I needed to devise a Plan. My problem was this: I knew, from my father, that pregnancy and children were the worst things that could possibly happen to you. What I didn't know was what caused pregnancy. I didn't know if it was something you could catch. I strongly suspected it could be something you ate. Right around that age, I became very careful about what I consumed. Basically I stuck to things I'd already tested. Eggs, for example, didn't do it. I knew 'cause I'd had lots of eggs and the unthinkable hadn't happened. Lobster, I wasn't going to try.

However, I felt I needed to have a Plan just in case it did happen to me. My Plan A was to kill myself. But then I needed a Plan B in case I didn't want to kill myself. Plan B in this case was to start wearing only my green paisley tent dress. It was the style that year . . . a dress with a high yoke and a very deep single pleat in front that could obscure any and all weight fluctuations. I would live in this dress and start carrying all my food into my room to eat. But I wouldn't eat it. None of it. So I would lose weight from not eating while I gained weight from pregnancy, and it would all even out. When the dreadful day arrived and the baby was going to come out, I'd go up in the woods, have the baby, kill it, and bury it. Luckily, having avoided lobster, I never had to enact either Plan A or Plan B.

We grew up very much alone in an old farmhouse in the middle of 148 acres. Mostly, my first five years were spent exclusively with my sister, my father, and my great aunt Martie. Then I started school, where I saw other kids for the first time. I hadn't seen children before. I didn't like them from the start. I never felt I was one of them. Why on earth would I want to produce one?

What would I have done with a baby? What if I'd had one when I was young and in college? What would have happened? How, from there, would I have grown up and become a stand-up comic and then a writer and a TV producer and a radio host? How could I have traveled the world from Europe to Africa and from Asia to Hawaii? I've worked on cruise ships and traipsed through refugee camps. I've traveled with international humanitarian aid groups, Medical Missions for Children, AmeriCares, and the Bridge Foundation, to hotspots and hellholes all around the world. In what, exactly, would I have packed the baby?

Life began at thirty when I started doing stand-up. I lived out of a suitcase. At the peak, I was logging forty-plus weeks a year on the road along with local weekends when I was in New York. Would I, being who I am, have been able to do all that and still find time to change dirty diapers? I have a strong gag reflex. I'm pretty sure they would have found me, dead, from choking to death during a Pampers explosion. I probably would have fallen face down, in it. It would have been a nasty CSI.

I couldn't do it. I couldn't have the kid. The specter of the physical side of it alone was enough to horrify me. A succubus growing and growing, consuming you from the inside until it erupts one day out of the smallest hole it can find. Good god. Women do this willingly? I'm not good with things living off other things. I don't even like seeing socks sticking to the sheets when they come out of the dryer.

The most appealing thing about having a kid is having them grow up and become younger adults who will visit you in the home. But it never felt right to me to have a baby just so I'd have somebody there to pull the plug. I would have needed to selflessly want to invest the twenty-odd years it would take to get them grown. I don't have a caretaker personality. I like to do what I want to do when I want to do it. It wouldn't have been fair.

In all this talk about my father, I haven't mentioned my mother. She left when I was one and a half. My first memory of her isn't till my early twos when for a while she came to take me on court-ordered visits on Sunday afternoons. My father told me a woman named Mrs. Willy was coming to see me. He was very clear in his instructions as to what I should call her. I should call her Mrs. Willy. Okay, I said. Sitting in the front seat of the car with her, with my legs so short not even my ankles hung off the front of the seat, she told me that she was my mother and that I could call her Mommy. I said, Okay, Mrs. Willy. She explained again that she was my mother. Okay, I said.

She could call herself whatever she liked. She had left before my earliest memory. I lived with my father and sister and great aunt all alone in that house with electricity in three rooms and heat in one, and there were no mothers there. We didn't have friends, neighbors, pets, or TV. I didn't know what a mother was. I still don't think I know. The whole "mother's unconditional love" thing? I don't get it. What does it look like; what does it feel like? I haven't the remotest idea. So how could I do it? I knew that if I had a baby, I might not love it right. She didn't. My mother didn't. I might leave it. I wasn't willing to have a baby and leave it, so I decided I wouldn't have one at any cost.

And besides, I knew from my own experience that it's no fun being born to ambivalence. I didn't know how I'd react to an actual you-can't-get-rid-of-it, baby. What if I didn't love it? What if I got sick of it? What if I hit it? And god knows what I'd be birthing that poor thing into. Life is wonderful and magical, and once you have it you hang onto it with everything you've got . . . but would you really wish it on a dog? Dying seems awful. Never existing? Not so sad.

The downside of not having children, other than dying alone after years of elder abuse in a state-run facility for people who get no visitors, is that you don't experience the circle. Through watching one's children grow, I think one comes to terms with one's own childhood. Things that didn't make sense then are poignant and bittersweet reexperienced through a daughter's first breakup or a son's tragic ouster from the football team. Full circle. A completion the childless don't get to have. People find meaning through knowing their children live on after them. I don't have future generations. I have to find my answers in impermanence. I'm looking for lasting meaning in a life that ends.

I feel I have to live more intensely and squeeze everything out of every moment so I can better stand it, years from now, lying on my death bed as alone in this world as it is possible to be. I will not be surrounded, as my father was, by daughters leaning over my bed talking me all the way to the veil. There will be no one to tell me I'm dying the right way. No one to tell me they love me and will love me forever.

I will be alone with my memories, reflective of a life lived for excitement and fulfillment. Experience is an end goal. At the finish, is it all going to be worth it? I have no idea. But I have lived a life that had no room for children. A life designed to give me memories for the end.

Did I ever tell you about the time I got booed offstage by Rangers—Special Service Rangers . . . large, large men? Armed men. I was doing stand-up on the DMZ in South Korea at the time. Or about the time I almost ran into a minefield in Kosovo weeks after the conflict ended? The buildings were still burning. Or how about that night in Brazzaville with Dr. Jamal who went back to Beirut shortly before the shelling began during that skirmish between Lebanon and Israel? We sat by the hotel pool with the smell of kerosene penetrating the air; it was late, but the doctor said, "How many nights will we all be together sitting like this with friends in Congo?" We stayed up until we killed that fifth of vodka.

I could spend my ending thinking about the time I flew to Germany to meet a stranger I found online. Or the time I was working cruise ships and the hurricane hit. Or the time I rode an elephant.

Or maybe I'll be thinking about all the lovely years with my wonderful boyfriend, Barry. (Turns out that whole relationship thing worked out after all. We've been together for sixteen years so far. He didn't want kids either.) Maybe I'll be thinking of him and me lounging on the back deck of the big house we could afford because we didn't have to send the cats to college. These are the memories that will comfort me as I gasp my last, lying alone and covered with bedsores in some nasty, pee-infested hell-pit of a nursing home.

In-Fertile Ground

Sue Kolinsky

If I had only known in my twenties how important it would be to have eggs in my forties, I would have stashed some away like people do on Easter.

To say that trying to get pregnant at forty-three is difficult is like saying the Mets had a chance of winning three in a row against the Yankees in the World Series. For those of you who don't appreciate a good baseball metaphor, it's like having the airline let you use your miles when you actually need them.

I began my baby-making journey at the precarious age of thirty-nine, a good year for finally understanding one's parents, but not so much for becoming one. I shared this adventure with my also-thirty-nine-but-going-on-twenty-year-old boyfriend. We had been together for twelve years by then and thought if we didn't have a kid soon, at some point we'd all be in diapers.

I remember so vividly our first attempt. It was down in Florida at his mom's, who (heavy Jewish accent) "had taken a place in Boca for the season." One night, in the TV/guest room we inhabited, he grabbed me as I was getting undressed, then asked with all the romance of a speed bump, "You wanna try to have a kid?" Caught off guard, I responded with an equally seductive, "I don't know. You wanna?" But once we set forth on our mission, that all changed. As we realized that we were creating a life, on its own and one together, our lovemaking became profound. Passionate! Omnipotent! I heard Handel's "Hallelujah."

The next morning I awoke with a smile and a craving for pickles and ice cream. I thought, *Wow! Does it really happen that fast?* No—unless you're seventeen, living at home, with a book report due. We soon learned the only thing we created that night was a spectacular memory, which we'd cling to in the months to come.

When you tell people you're trying to get pregnant they say, "That's great! You must be having sex all the time." Well, we were having something, but it bore little resemblance to the sex we knew. It was now dictated by rules and regulations. Passion took a backseat to dates, charts, and pee. Sex had quite simply become a chore. I recall several occasions when my former hot-to-trot partner turned to me, pleading, "Do we have to? Can't we do it later?" He even resorted to making deals like, "If we do it tomorrow, I'll walk the dog, too." Having an orgasm wasn't good enough. Now you had to go for the two-point conversion. And every time you didn't succeed, you felt like the kid at the carnival playing that crane game, feverishly trying to win the toy he can never quite grasp. The pressure is greater when you're running out of quarters.

We tried for a year. Nothing. I was forty, and my biological clock had become Big Ben. We took the next step and met with a fertility doctor. He came highly recommended by a good friend, whose selling point was that the doc was once a minor league ballplayer in the Met's organization. I liked him already. Apparently, he didn't have what it took to make it to "The Show," so he traded in his leather gloves for latex. As we stepped into his office, the baby pictures lining the walls told us he was finally batting well over 500. We were optimistic. Excited.

During our first visit, we sat with him for almost two hours as he explained the procedures we needed in our attempt to produce our "little miracle." The first was temperature-taking every morning with a basal thermometer, a device ultra sensitive to the body's minutest change in temperature. I felt like I was making a turkey. I was then to immediately note the data on a graph to chart the rise and fall of degrees. If my temperature continued to climb over the course of a couple of days, I was at the gates of ovulation land—which, in retrospect, should have had a sign: "ENTER AT YOUR OWN RISK."

If this method fails, it's time to purchase an ovulation kit, which basically provides cups to pee in. At least I wouldn't have to label them with my name, unless for some reason there were other women in my house trying to get pregnant by my boyfriend, in which case trying to conceive wasn't my biggest problem. The "sample" is then placed in a plastic applicator that houses two small horizontal lines, one on top of the other. After five minutes, if the bottom line appears darker than the one above, it's off to the races to gather sperm in yet another cup to be brought to the doctor within *one hour* for insemination. And of course, before doing all this . . . RELAX!

When we arrive at the doctor's office with our cup o' sperm, it's taken for a ride in a carousel of sorts for about an hour, where it's washed and checked for mobility. If the little fellows can master the art of the backstroke, or any stroke for that matter, it's time for their close-up inside me.

When the doctor told us what the sperm has to go through to fertilize the egg, it's a miracle anyone gets pregnant. It has to swim up a canal, climb over the uterine wall, and shoot a rifle. What is this? An Iron Man competition?

And sometimes the little swimmer loses its bearings and ends up in the bladder. I picture the egg holding up a map, telling the sperm he's not even in the uterus. "Maybe we should ask some of this scar tissue because that tunnel back there looked really familiar." Of course sperm, being masculine, refuse to ask for directions.

After insertion, I lie there in my sexy paper gown with my legs bent and up in the air for fifteen minutes. I'm trying to think positive thoughts—as well as begging God to forgive me for the jacket I stole from Macy's when I was sixteen. It didn't work.

With each failed attempt, the pressure to succeed was mounting. With conventional methods not working, I decided to explore the world of "alternative." I went for acupuncture twice a week. I even boiled and drank the stinky herbs, trying not to gag at the most disgusting combination of odor and taste anyone should have to endure for anything. I came back from the health food store with a bevy of vitamins, whole grains, and organic fruits and vegetables. I started taking yoga—thinking if all of this didn't work, I'd be limber enough to actually go inside my body and check on things myself.

After years of trying every method known to God, man, and science, with no result, I was losing my resolve. Tired of asking, "Who do you have to fuck to have a baby around here," I slumped onto the couch, grabbed the remote, and flipped through channels. I stopped at an episode of *Cops,* taken by the image on the screen. There's this forty-year-old overweight woman, puffing on a Marlboro, with a can of beer in one hand and three of her fifteen kids in the other. A light bulb went off in my head. Apparently, the egg has a far better chance of enticing the sperm in the midst of unsavory activity and shitty conditions.

So now, after fifteen inseminations and nothing to show for it (except a large co-payment), I am married to a man who has had a vasectomy, and quite happy that my dog will remain an only child.

No Free Babysitter

Jane Gennaro

My mother likes to tell us kids, "I never really cared if I had children." If we ask why she had six of us, she says, "It was a complete love affair with your father." Four of us were born in November, nine months after Valentine's Day, which makes me think my mother could be had for a box of chocolates with nuts. Mom has a taste for sharing salty tidbits, like when "Dad was down in the dumps" she'd do something with red wine to "perk him up" and, one summer day while we were splashing in the backyard swimming pool, she and Dad were doing it "standing up in the pantry"; even as an adult, I would rather stick my nose under the smelly mildew pool lining and lick a squished slug than picture that.

Mary and Jay were popular and gave great parties, which we were allowed to stay up for in our nice pajamas, to serve the grown-ups pigs in a blanket, with toothpicks standing in a shot glass, Gulden's mustard, and cocktail napkins. The longer we stayed up, the more likely the chance one of us would be asked to go to the stereo and flip the LP record *Alley Cat/Green Onions* to side two and drop the needle on Henry Mancini's "The Stripper," so Mom could do her "number," which I guess you'd call a bump and grind, with Mom's signature sound effect: a *cluck cluck* mouth noise on the pelvic thrust.

The joyful thing about having children is you can make them do things for you like put on your music, or bring you a Manhattan, or rub your back. (Dad paid a dime for five minutes and a quarter for unlimited.) On the *down* side, you have to do things for *them*, like feed them and clothe them and, worse, *watch* them—or pay somebody else to, unless you're able to solicit volunteers. My mother always told us, "If you have kids, don't count on me to babysit." This was helpful information when I was in fifth grade, planning my future and weighing the pros and cons of my two vocations—I wanted to be a nun or a veterinarian and marry Little Joe Cartwright or God, depending—but I wasn't sure if I was supposed to have children, so I started a list called REASONS TO *HAVE* OR *NOT HAVE* KIDS, and entered "No free babysitter" in the *NOT HAVE* column.

Despite Mom's earthy annunciations and artful burlesques, the birds and the bees remained a mystery in our house, save for the curious clue that popped out unexpectedly, like the morning Dad sat down to a Saturday breakfast of French toast and bacon, unaware his bathrobe was open and his PJ bottoms were not fully snapped, prompting Mom to stage-whisper, "Jay, your *doodads!*" Or the time I panicked, "Mom come quick! Sampson's intestines are falling out!' and was mortified to be reassured the moist red thing emerging like a slug from our cocker spaniel puppy was merely a male dog's "business."

As teenagers, Mom warned us, "Never kiss in a reclining position," but we were not brought up to be the kind of children who would think of asking, "Where do babies come from?" Besides, I *knew* babies came from the hospital, like milk and eggs come from the grocery store. Every so often, mom would go to the hospital and come back with a baby, like a loaf of bread. Mary would be the first to tell you, "I have taste and style," and so I never really associated her sartorial proclivity for the crisply ironed A-line blouse with there being anything of particular interest beneath it, except perhaps "a good eye."

REASON TO HAVE KIDS: fashion statement
REASON TO NOT HAVE KIDS: fashion statement

The word *pregnant* was not uttered in our house. Mom called it "expecting." Alas, expectations lead to disappointment. When Ellen was born, she assumed she was the only child and expected to have my parents all to herself forever, but eleven months later, I came along usurping her "new baby" status and giving us a shared identity as what Mom called Irish Twins. Little did we know, we were paving the way for the onslaught of siblings to come, each one of us bent on creating a unique way to grab the spotlight of our parents' attention, which is why people describe us as "artistic."

REASON TO HAVE KIDS: kids think their parents are the center of the universe
REASON TO NOT HAVE KIDS: kids realize their parents are not the center of the universe

My mother always said, "Children are a gift from God." If children are a gift from God, atheism would be a form of birth control. Our great atheist forefather Benjamin Franklin produced not only the lightning rod, lending library, and bifocals, but a couple of offspring as well. Even Freud, a committed nonbeliever, was a prolific breeder of six children. Besides, if children are a gift, how come you can't return them? Or donate your colicky tot to the PTA Elephant Sale? The Salvation Army won't take away your bullying kindergartner, anorexic-shoplifting tweenie, or sulky suicidal teenager, even if it's stuck to a really great sofa.

REASON TO NOT HAVE KIDS: you have to keep them

But who says you're supposed to *have* them? Okay, the pope, but even Catholics are allowed to practice "rhythm," a method of birth control that explains why all six kids my mother gave birth to within nine years were born able to keep a beat.

REASON TO HAVE KIDS: children can be entertaining

Full Disclosure: I'm not a mother, but I've played perky moms on TV commercials, so I know something about it. My TV children were professionally adorable, reliably rambunctious rug rats reeling off their résumés with practiced smiles before their real moms could beat them to it. A number of those pint-size grown-ups worked a hell of a lot more than I did! You don't have be Snow White's evil stepmother to be jealous of your kid. I can only imagine it's worse with the real kind. I'd especially hate to have a daughter who was "Daddy's little girl." Yuck.

REASON TO NOT HAVE KIDS: husband might love them more than you

No doubt, I'd be throwing the temptress-toddler straight into Daddy's arms by refusing to give the requisite "fairy princess party" and dressing the little vixen in a smart double-breasted navy wool suit with a pleated skirt and mother-of-pearl buttons—like mom dressed us four little girls in, including one-year-old baby Martha—as opposed to the uniform pink tutu, strap-on wings, and glitter tiara condoned by the current mother-cult, who power-push Hummer-like three-across baby strollers down city sidewalks on a mission for overpriced gelato, Gymboree, and "Mommy and Me" pedicures; followed by the seizure and occupation of communal apartment hallways for personal use as parking spaces for baby vehicles, discarded Diaper.com boxes, and Fresh Direct pickups.

REASON TO HAVE KIDS: entitlement

"Marry a Jew!" was perhaps uncommon advice coming from my Irish Catholic mother, but from what she'd seen at the First Investors' office party—besides Marty the Clown stretching crazy animal balloons for the kiddies; an astonishing array of deli salads, pickles, and platters piled high with thick sandwiches stuck through with cellophane-ruffled toothpicks; and Dad and Quigley, the two gentiles in the company, joking about being members of the Token Christians Club—she concluded, "Those Jewish husbands treat their wives like princesses!" And while I did land my own personal Jew, our mutual attraction transcended religion. Stephen fell for my ample maternal bosom.

REASON TO NOT HAVE KIDS: breastfeeding

I fell for Stephen's weight-lifter physique, plus the fact he was a psychologist. How many men can take a load off your mind and carry it on their shoulders?

REASON TO HAVE KIDS: good genes
REASON TO NOT HAVE KIDS: girl might get his nose, boy might get my boobs

My mother refers to Stephen as "My son-in-law, the only Jewish doctor who doesn't make money." Fortunately, I was not prone to cupidity or longing for maternity when we got married, so the idea of having a ton of money or a tiny tot fit snugly in the drawer of "remote possibilities" for the first ten years of our marriage, during which time we had apparently been brainwashed by the zeitgeist, because the eleventh year of our union erupted in the embedded vision and heinous concept of a "biological clock" ticking. It's one thing to say you don't care about something while the opportunity to obtain it is still available to you. It's another thing to suddenly notice how much stuff comes stamped with an expiration date. Thus, Stephen and I found ourselves revisiting the possibility of parenthood.

STEPHEN: My preference is to be a broken limb (his father's metaphor for couples without children), but if you want to I will.
JANE: Hot potato!
STEPHEN: You need to decide by the time you're thirty-seven, because after that I'm going to be too old to deal with kids.
JANE: What if I told you I was expecting right now?
STEPHEN: (look of terror)
JANE: I mean, I wonder if me really wanting something would make you want it too.

STEPHEN: I just want you to be happy.

JANE: That's such a Jewish-husband thing to say! Thank you, honey.

Funny how ambivalence can enhance romance and trigger that old "first dating" spontaneity but with even less precaution. That's dangerous. How sexy! Or was it just us entering into a cowardly contract to let the fates decide? Perhaps I was fueled by the fear I'd be missing out on something wonderful if we never had children. Maybe Stephen's subconscious was propelling him to satisfy his parent's desire for grandchildren. Whatever. Lusting after destiny's decision was an erotic escape from the tiresome maneuvers of reality. Oh, what rapture realized assuming exotic positions! How unlike harried married couples whose sex lives had been forever dampened by the demands of parenthood! Unless . . . what if our sudden Let's Get It On gluttony was actually some sort of mythic send-off of exploding fireworks choreographed by the gods? A last-gasp binge of unequivocal ecstasy, ordained to be exchanged for the bliss or misery that only having children can bestow? A proper orgy is a matter of life and death. As mere mortals, our greatest drives are to reproduce and avoid death. Still, confronting your own mortality is such a downer. We came up for air. *Who will take care of us in our old age?* Had *that* banality been the impetus for our happy hump fest? I heard the plaintive plea of my book club buddy Cindy. "Who is going to be around to see me though the next twenty years?" she'd asked and answered as quickly, "Certainly not my daughters, who are put out when they even have to answer the door when I've forgotten my key!"

REASON TO HAVE KIDS: 50-50 chance they'll take care of you in your old age.

REASON TO NOT HAVE KIDS: 50-50 chance they'll take care of you in your old age.

I hate being asked, "Do you have children?" especially by people who have them, because as soon as I answer "No," I'm assaulted by an almost imperceptible pregnant pause, rudely begging explanation. I pull from my stock of caveats that start with: "I love kids, but . . ."

- I don't want to be disappointed on Mother's Day.
- I refuse to be limited to minivans.
- I'd eat all the Ritalin.
- I don't want to inflict long-term psychological damage on lice.
- Stephen and I refuse to contribute to the world's overpopulation crisis.

Okay, that last one's a joke. I'm ashamed to admit qualms about the destruction of the planet were never a real consideration in our decision, but you'd think by now the human instinct to procreate would have evolved enough to grasp "mission accomplished" and just come in waves, or alternate generations. I mean, we pretty much rule the Earth with the ants, and it's no picnic, but our therapist had actually said it was people like Stephen and me who *should* be having children, which was a rare courageous statement of personal opinion, considering the crenels of history contain many tales of shrinks beheaded for using the word "should." Plus, her statement was sooo elitist it made me feel superior! I will always love her for that.

REASON TO HAVE KIDS: to please your therapist

As a kid, I resented homework. Now I hear myself say, "Just give me my homework," hoping if I follow instructions carefully, and answer all the questions, I'll come up with the correct answer. But the baby question has no right or wrong answer because it's different for everybody. I hate that! Determined to obtain deeper insight into Stephen's *male* perspective, I thought to poll all men in general, but narrowed the field to "men with jobs" and started asking strangers, "Do you think I should have a baby?"

BUS DRIVER: Yes!
CAB DRIVER: You are woman, no?
MAILMAN: I would like to be the father.

Finally, I asked my brother Mark, who didn't get what the problem was. "You always *know* what you want," he said. "So if you *don't know*, you probably *don't want* it." Mom has always said, "That Jane does exactly what she wants," only it isn't a compliment.

"I'm late!" I confided to my friend Barbie, walking on the beach. I had spotted a small red stone and was holding it pressed to my palm. "Really?" Barb's immediate fascination and loaded inflection hung in the salty air, equally weighted between statement and question. Then suddenly I arced my arm back and catapulted the bloody talisman into the ocean. Decision made! And confirmed the next day by the arrival of my period.

"Why is *period* so much nicer than *menses?*" Stephen mused.

"*Menses* sounds like *Mensa*," I said, even though saying *menses* makes me cringe. "There's an intelligence to it, like a living creature," I said.

"Whereas 'period' has a finality to it," continued Stephen, "like *you're not having a kid, period!*"

He gently removed a chilled cocktail glass from the freezer, poured in an autumnal-colored mixture from his stainless steel cocktail shaker, popped in a maraschino cherry, and handed me my Manhattan. "From now on when people ask, 'Do you have children?' I'm just going to say, 'No,' period." I said, swallowing that luscious first cool sip, and feeling like my mother who likes to remind her children, "I never made my kids say they were sorry when they weren't." I watched the cherry sink slowly toward the bottom of my glass.

First Comes Love

Laurie Graff

D *ebbie and Teddy sittin' in a tree, K-I-S-S-I-N-G.*
It was the summer we turned sixteen she first started to
talk about it. We were upstate in the Catskills, at the bun-
galow colony, and Debbie's mother had asked her to hang the wash
out to dry. If handing Debbie the clothespins counts, I was helping.
And between you and me, I was pretty annoyed about it too. Why, on
a beautiful Saturday afternoon, smack in the middle of our summer
vacation, did Debbie have to deal with her family's laundry? Wasn't
that her mother's job? In our house, it was. But she was my best summer friend, and I promised to wait for her to go to the pool, so I was
stuck. And to make matters worse, all Debbie wanted to talk about was
her wedding.

"It'll be in a church, of course. There'll be a long procession, and my father will walk me down the aisle, and I'll be dressed in lace, all in white," she explained, grabbing one of her mother's bras and efficiently attaching it to the makeshift clothesline. "I'm not sure yet about the bouquets, but I know it'll be in winter because I want all my brides-maids to wear velvet. Red velvet. Doesn't that sound beautiful? Maybe we'll get married around the same time, Laurie! What color dresses will your bridesmaids wear?"

What color . . . ? "I have no idea," I said. "I never thought about it."

"Oh. Well, where do you want your wedding to be?" she asked.

"Who knows?"

"But don't you dream about it? Don't you dream about getting married as soon as you get out of school?"

It was more like the last thing I dreamt about. I dreamt about freedom. And travel. I dreamt a whole lot about acting. And much ado about dating.

First comes love—

"Well, as soon as I get out of college, I'm going to buy a red Volkswagen bug, drive cross-country to Los Angeles, start my career, and star in a sitcom," I announced, surprising myself with the drama of the car when, a city girl through and through, I knew my career would begin in New York.

The winter we were twenty-two, I missed Debbie's wedding because I was in Detroit. Playing the Fisher Theatre. Performing as "Frenchy" in the national tour of the hit musical *Grease*. My friend sent me photographs; the red velvet was beautiful, and Deb's white dress was, indeed, made of lace.

Then comes marriage—

But all my friends now were theater people. Even my cousins act and write, so to me the world was divided into two groups: the civilians, and *us*. The civilians would be the ones to marry, breed, and move to the burbs. The rest of us would stay in the city and keep up the cultured, creative life. It was an unspoken agreement, and nary the two worlds would dare intertwine. I kept my part of the bargain. And make no mistake about it, I felt sure we all made one.

Years rolled by, and all my friends led similar lives. One by one we each left roommates to rent on our own. Like in a small town, we'd run into each other at appointments and classes, people going from gig to gig, the circles widening as people worked with friends of friends, slept with friends of friends. Who's who? Auditions and agents, boyfriends and breakups, we'd talk on the phone and meet up for meals.

So, more than a little thrown, I actually felt betrayed when Jenny, my girlfriend from summer stock who got me out of my mother's apartment in Queens and into my own room (albeit what was once the maid's quarters) as one of four roommates in a Classic Six, my first New York apartment, told me . . . there was this guy. We were in Carl Schurz Park. It was a hot day, and I felt like I was dissolving. The clarity of Jenny's actions was so big it absorbed all the uncertainty of my own. It was the first time I was seeing her since I'd returned to New York after a six-month stint living in Los Angeles. Toying with the idea of moving out. Hoping Jenny might come too.

She stared me down as if I had returned from California and grown another head. Didn't I get her letter? Did she not write she had met a guy on her vacation to Jamaica? And didn't she tell me that she was in love?

"Well, yes, of course you did. And I wrote you back. I remember everything you said about Billy. He's like in construction or something, right? And he lives like someplace, someplace not the city? Right? So yes, I remember what you said. And I assumed by now you'd broken up."

But Jenny had not broken up. On the contrary, she thought he was it. Jenny was moving in. Up there! She was going to live with him in Westchester County. Tarrytown. And if marriage wasn't enough, Jenny was leaving acting and taking a job in sales. She was becoming a commuter. All to save money. Buy a house. And—

Then comes a baby in the baby carriage!

A baby. We weren't even thirty. Why in the world would anyone want to stop her life to have a baby? To my great surprise, it seemed a lot of women did.

"Well that's normal," my mother explained. "You meet someone, you marry, you have a baby, and you make a life. That's what you call a normal life," my mother would say.

Except it wasn't hers. My mother's normal turned out to be that of a woman who was a pioneer of divorce in the early sixties. And, by example, it wasn't mine. No, my role model, single working mom, nose to the unending grindstone, did not even date until I went off to college, working full-time in order to support my younger brother and me. My mother endured what seemed like endless drudgery. So tell me. If that's normal, who in the world would want to duplicate it?

All right, I know. It doesn't have to be that way. Not everyone gets divorced. Besides, coming of age after the women's movement, I was told I could have it all. Forget the Costco life. Mine could be different. And with the right man, mine could include a kid, a co-op, *and* a career in the city. With the right man. Except I didn't meet him.

Oh, there were men. Men with whom I shared love affairs that included many a color of many a rainbow. But none with whom I could paint my picture. Yet I have come to believe that for many women, having a child is their picture. And they have learned to paint by numbers in order to create it.

Some years ago I was attracted to a man who said he was leaving his wife, but I would not enable it by his cheating with me. I bowed out. As I had turned a little more than the corner on forty, several friends suggested I harvest my eggs.

"What if you don't meet anyone else and then he comes back and it's too late? You don't want him going to someone else just because she's younger."

Of all the scenarios, I didn't know which was harder to imagine. That he would really leave his wife. That he'd come back. That I would actually harvest my eggs, or that I would not be enough for him without them.

Eighteen months later, he called to say he was divorced, hopeful now we would really be together. Playing for keeps, I took it very slow. Apparently too slow, because at the point I was ready to open my heart he announced it was quits. He didn't plan it but, well, things just happen, and he didn't know how it happened but somehow he just began, well, schtupping someone else. His duplicity felt devastating.

Then one day, a year later, I was with Jenny at a restaurant in Grand Central Station. All dressed up we were celebrating my baby, the publication of my very first novel. She and I had not seen each other in a while, and I was bringing her up to speed. As if he were a living illustration, who was suddenly standing next to our table?

Last I had seen him, I was throwing his briefcase down the hall before slamming the door to my apartment behind him. Now, here he was. Congratulating, as he had seen my book everywhere. Asking if I had become a millionaire yet. Telling me how he had made a mistake. And promising me he was going to call.

"Oh my God," said Jenny. "That's him, that's the guy? He's adorable. And he's a successful news producer. Get him before someone else does. Marry him. I say go for it."

Go for it? Wasn't Jenny listening? "I could never . . ." There were a whole bunch of reasons why I'd never marry him, and I bulleted them all out.

"So what?" she said, pooh-poohing away potential disaster. "You can always get divorced. At least you'll get a baby."

"I'm not trying to get a baby. I'm trying to get the love."

"Well," said Jenny. "Isn't that love?"

Don't worry. This is not where I go and get all sentimental. A baby may be love, but it is not romantic love. A baby is not a partner. A person with needs, its care and feeding, is not the same as a pet. It is a life that deserves to begin its journey in a home with two parents who are in love. And not just with the baby, but each other. Untraditional families aside, and not that there's anything wrong with that, I will tell you, as I watch the trade-offs people make, that I no longer believe everyone starts out that way. I no longer believe that everyone who is married has fallen in love, or even wanted to. And that's okay. For them.

People set out with the best of intentions. But I do think many people connect by connecting the dots to paint their big picture. And in the center of their canvas is a child. No matter what happens, they will always feel it was all worth it, because first and foremost they are thrilled to be a parent, thrilled to have that child. If I'm not sure this is true, I can ask (too) many friends. Hey, I can just ask my mom.

Most recently I had a date with a man who, like me, never married. In talking about his nephew, he told me a big regret was that he had never had children. "It's a great burden that I take through life," he confessed of being childless.

He felt it was his moral duty to propagate. As he has not, he will not pass that legacy on. However, a Pulitzer Prize–nominated journalist and author, he has created quite a legacy of a different sort. Would he have accomplished those goals if he had been hell-bent to never miss a soccer game? Would he have been able to do it all? Or would he have gone to the games with resentment, knowing he was no longer free to travel the world for months at a time?

"True," he said, "nothing is perfect. Although there was that one woman . . ." The rest of the sentence drifted into the utopian world of if only.

At one time, just imagined, the road less traveled can now be viewed on Facebook. When I look at Facebook, I am a voyeur. I see pictures, happy pictures of the families my peers have created. I see the choices of girlfriends while piecing together the lives of ex-boyfriends. Artists and civilians alike, divorced, married, widowed, single, straight, or gay, they update their status and show off their kids. I do not know how they really feel, but it looks picture perfect. I look at those perfect pictures, and I feel a pang.

Now I will let you in on something about me. That pang is about feeling out of step with the stages of life more than of having missed out on them. This is not to say that I haven't, for maybe I have, but I have also been too busy to notice. Good, bad; up, down; I continue to stay the course. Still part of the non-civilian *us,* still in the city, I still continue the pursuit of my dreams. It's who I am and how I live. My life, my own; I have not passed the baton. The best, I believe, is still yet to come.

Aha, Ha Ha

Carol Siskind

I have chosen not to study Latin.
   I have chosen not to drink bourbon.
   And I have chosen not to have children.

On my thirtieth birthday, too many years ago, my mother said, "Y'know, you don't have to be married to have a baby."

I thought, "How hip and modern she is." And she was. Well, I guess I was modern too, because my first thought was, "Who wants a baby?" It's not something I'd ever pictured for myself. I was content spending my waking moments thinking, reading, writing, and performing stand-up comedy. My career was already thriving, with some TV, lots of press, as well as great "spots" at the best clubs in New York City. My parents had seen me perform more than once. Was this her way of saying, "Get a day job?"

Interesting that this came from her, because she was an artist. While she didn't make a living from her art, she exceeded at painting, crocheting, needlework, and eventually sculpting. She was always making something. What she left behind for us to enjoy is truly remarkable, in skill and output.

She would always say she was "born too soon."

She'd also say, "Marry a pilot; they're never home."

It was obvious that she felt her domestic obligations kept her from pursuing an independent, creative life more seriously.

I can't know if she was cut out for the total commitment of an artist in her day. But I knew what she wanted for me. Having it all, bigger than big. Better than better. Yes, where she couldn't, I could.

I fell into doing stand-up after meeting a gal at an acting audition who told me she was a comedian. A light bulb moment, bells-and-whistles worthy. I went with her to an obscure off-off-off-Broadway cabaret. I got up, told a story off the cuff, got some laughs, and never looked back.

So, Mom, I thought, *Baby? Comedy is my baby. And how blessed am I to find this baby, a passion I could never have imagined.*

It isn't like I didn't have kids in my life. My darling sister-in-law, Mary Ann, whom I met when I was fifteen, let me share in her children's lives so completely, so generously, that her kids were my kids. I have loved them as my own. Maybe that's not possible, but for me it's been everything.

I was fully involved with them whenever I could be, but happily left them all in the suburbs to return to my club family in the City, where I'd do a set. Or up to six sets, depending on how many clubs I wanted to hit that night.

Was I too selfish? Was I too immature? Was I too frightened? I don't think so. Having children was never on my radar. Being married wasn't either. I thought if I met the right guy, maybe it would change. But it never did. One dinner date I had before going to a club said "This comedy is just a hobby, right?" Never saw him again.

Another, a blind date, dropped me off at a club after dinner. A few nights later, when I entered that club, the manager said, "Someone's here for you." Then I heard him, his loud voice coming from the showroom, where he was loudly heckling the MC. I peeked in, saw my boor of a date, and then, horrified, bolted for home. I guess a lot of people want to be comedians.

Comedy came first, before anything else. In the first six years of doing stand-up, I think I missed only thirty nights. I wanted to get good at it, so I got up in front of an audience anytime I could. In the beginning that might mean Central Park (with a couple of guys and a guitar case), the back room of a New York City fortune teller, or a Soho loft party. I was willing to humiliate myself over and over in order to improve.

I was driven. I didn't long for another life. I was thrilled with this one. I loved the clubs, hanging out with funny and, surprisingly, not so funny comics. While I treasured the relationship I had with my brother and his family, I never pictured that for myself. I was consumed with doing everything in my power to see if I had what it took to carve out a career as a professional comedian. This still is so significant to me. A challenge, a love, a protector, a source of pride, self-esteem, joy, and fulfillment.

Is this what good parenting feels like? I guess I've parented myself in a way. I've reprimanded myself to do my writing homework. I've encouraged myself to go on when jokes bomb. I've let myself feel good when I've shone in the harsh business of show.

So here, we arrive at my "aha" moment:

A few months into performing, I bombed horribly in a small club in New York City called Good Times. It wasn't "good times" for me. I was so awful, so bad, that I cleared the room. Oh, the horror.

On my walk of shame home, and up to my fifth-floor walk-up, I thought to myself, verbatim, *Carol, you are going back there tomorrow night. You will get right back on that stage, no matter how impossible that seems right now. Because if you don't, you are never doing stand-up again. If you don't dig down and find the guts to go back, know this: You will never, ever again be able to watch another comedian on TV or anywhere else. You will be so filled with remorse and disappointment in yourself. You will regret this for the rest of your life.*

I got myself back there the next night, and every night thereafter. Did I have bad sets after that night? Sure, but I knew what the stakes were for me, and I did not want to live out my life with that kind of regret.

Sure I could have had children *and* had a career as a comedian. Some do. But I don't think I would've done either one that well. Not me. Maybe others, but not me. Not in the all-encompassing, neurotic, totally obsessed way that I choose to do things that I truly love.

I've been lucky in my life. My loving parents and family (once they got over the "What is she doing now?" reaction) supported me and came to countless shows into the wee hours. I've also been blessed to meet and perform with some of the most fantastic, inspiring, and funny people on Planet Earth.

So, had I not dragged my ass back to Good Times the night after I mega-ton bombed, today I would be living in overwhelming regret. And this is the thing. Honestly, I have never felt that regret whenever I've seen a diaper, stroller, cloth bathtub book, or child. I feel full. Not just from overeating, which I do on a regular basis. I feel full when I am onstage entertaining people. And I feel full when I see my nieces and nephews parent their own precious kids. Sharing the lives of these little ones gives me great joy. But making people laugh goes to the core of who I am—and how fabulous it is for me that I'm able to do it.

I feel I should end with a joke, so here's one I wrote years ago.

IT'S SERIOUS BUSINESS HAVING CHILDREN.

BEFORE YOU DO, GO VISIT DISNEY WORLD.

YOU'LL FIND THOUSANDS OF KIDS ACTING LIKE BRATS.

IT'S WILD. REALLY. I SWEAR I SAW THE POPE THERE, HANDING OUT CONDOMS.

Now, readers, go forward and multiply. Do it for those of us who've chosen not to. And many thanks.

Without Issue

Bernadette Luckett

I never had kids, but I love them. I really do. Especially when they're babies. I'm one of those people who compulsively talks to every baby I see on the street, in stores, anywhere. I talk to babies and dogs. I don't have a dog either.

Babies are pure, sweet, and innocent. It's always about truth with them because they haven't yet learned how to ease social situations with a fake smile or feigned interest. A baby's never told me I look fat, or tired, or asked where I'm working. I like that. If I go to a party and there's a baby there, I'll beeline to the baby for some easygoing, authentic company. I'm actually happiest going to a party if there are only babies there. But babies rarely throw parties without dragging along adults who like to machine-gun nonreproductive oddities like me, shooting us with quips about our aging eggs and asking, "How come you don't have kids?" It seems by now I'd have some snappy response to that question, something quick, carefree, and simple. When in truth, the answer to that question is far from simple.

If I look back at my life, I've had some wonderful experiences being around babies. Once, I was on a spiritual retreat in Ireland, and we went to visit a sacred site. There was a huge labyrinth there, and I decided to walk it. Halfway through, a woman carrying a six-month-old baby came nearby. I noticed them and waved at the baby. The woman, taking this as an invitation, walked across the labyrinth to talk to me. That's pretty much the way it is in Ireland, you look at someone and they'll talk to you, and talk to you, and tell you stories until your ears drop off. As she stood there, her red-haired baby leaned over to me with her hands outstretched. The mother smiled and cheerfully said, "Go ahead and take her." So I reached out and took the baby.

She sat up in my arms happily, then all of a sudden she leaned into me and rested her head against my chest. It took me by surprise. I continued to hold her while I talked to the mother about I-don't-remember-what. When the mother was ready to go, she called out the baby's name and reached out to take her from me. The baby lifted her head, looked at her mother, then held me tightly and placed her head back on my chest. Both the mother and I laughed in awkward embarrassment and contin-ued a slightly more tense I-don't-remember-what conversation. After a minute or so, the baby again lifted her head, reached out her arms, and went back to her mother. We said good-bye, and they left. I turned back to continue on the labyrinth, took one step, and burst into tears. I don't even know why. I just knew that my heart, my whole chest, was on fire. At that moment I wanted a baby. No . . . I wanted *that* baby. Unfortu-nately, when I looked up, the mother and baby were out of sight, and the opportunity to negotiate a sale was gone.

I've read about women who are consumed with wanting a baby. All I can remember ever being consumed with wanting is . . . a chemistry set, toe shoes, and to marry Ringo. Perhaps I just wasn't born with that maternal thing that makes a woman want to pop out a child.

I did have maternal instincts though. I had dolls when I was young. I had a black doll. When she fell dangerously close to the floor heater, her skin began to peel off. Under the dark rubbery surface layer of skin, she was a white doll. I was fascinated. I began peeling away at the dark layer of skin on her face and legs. Some of it came off, and some of it didn't. She turned into a spotty mess. But I loved her anyway. I was a good mother to my sweet little vitiligo'd baby doll.

And even when I was twelve, my neighbor Rhonda and I used to pretend we were pushing baby strollers down the street. We both knew every detail about our pretend babies: their names, what they were wearing, what they liked to eat and didn't. My baby, Tina, occasionally peed, and I had to pretend to change her diaper. But she never pooped. I guess I didn't even have it in me to deal with pretend poop. I wasn't the best mother to my constipated pretend baby, but I did the best I could. I guess all mothers do the best they can.

But sometimes I wonder if maybe I was influenced by my mother's attitude about having children.

Having kids was something my mother didn't always handle well. She was a great mother in most respects; I mean she fed me, combed my hair, took care of me when I was sick, all that caring mother stuff. But when pushed beyond her emotional tolerance, she could say the meanest things. And I must admit I had some perverse pleasure in pushing her to that point of irrational expletive. Her anger would rise, her eyes would narrow, her lips would purse, and she'd spit out at me with enough intensity to chill my bones, "I shoulda pinched your little head off when you were coming out!" This both frightened and confused me, because the first few times she said it, I didn't really know where babies came from. Where was I coming out of, and how were you going to pinch my head off? Later, the thought of being decapitated by some quick, enraged kegel-esque move proved pretty disturbing to me. Still, I like to repaint that memory of my mother and just chalk it up to her having an uncensored and wickedly creative way of expressing herself. Though I wonder at times if what she said had some deep unconscious effect on me. That it put out a message to me that children were trouble, something to be regretted.

That message was confirmed with the 1960s film *Village of the Damned*. In a small town in England, everything stopped one day. All the people and animals mysteriously collapsed and were out for hours. When they awoke, all the women of childbearing age were pregnant. In less than nine months, the babies were born on the same night, with similar looks: white-blond hair and piercing blue eyes. As they grew, it became evident they had unnatural abilities. They would stare at people, and their alien blue eyes would light up, and the people they were staring at would commit suicide—with shotguns, and fire, and by driving cars into walls. Very nasty stuff. The children were evil and had to be destroyed. But they could read your mind. Oh my God, how were they going to save themselves when these evil children could read their minds?!

That movie gave me nightmares well into my teens. And although I love children, that particular combination of white-blond hair and blue eyes still makes me a bit uncomfortable. In fact, while strolling through a botanical garden in Copenhagen one summer, I just about spit out my Jolly Cola as I came upon a group of Danish school children—all white-haired and blue-eyed. I held my breath, kept my mind blank, and moved slowly out of the area, being careful not to look at them or vex them in any possible way lest I be immediately targeted by their deadly stares, causing me to hurl myself into the lily pond and drown.

But surely my own children wouldn't be evil. And, being black, there's very little chance they'd have white-blonde hair and blue eyes.

So what else could've happened to influence me about having children? A lingering fear of pregnancy.

I attended an all-girls Catholic high school, where the nuns drilled the fear of pregnancy into us. You weren't even supposed to stand next to a guy wearing patent leather shoes because he might use them as mirrors to look up your skirt. I didn't know how, but there was some way, as I understood it, that could get you pregnant. Or, if you sat on a boy's lap without placing a telephone book there first, that sneaky sperm lurking somewhere inside his mysterious hanging man parts would find its way up to your uterus and make you pregnant. I had a few pieces of the sexuality puzzle put together, but I didn't have the top of the box with the full picture.

I remember as a child being shocked beyond belief when the kids across the street, who knew everything about everything, told me that "fuck," that bad word graffiti'ed on a neighborhood wall, was what Mommy and Daddy did to make babies. I didn't believe them. No way! I pored through our *Encyclopedia Britannica* looking for the truth. Under the heading "Sexual Reproduction," I found out how birds do it, cows do it, and frogs do it, but there was nothing to explain how humans did it, nor was there any mention of the word "fuck."

I was woefully naive and sexually ignorant, but no more than my older sister, who thought you could get pregnant just by dancing close to a guy. After her junior prom, she spent three weeks terrified that she was "in a family way." Having a baby was the worst possible thing that could happen to a nice, unmarried, Catholic girl. And when you didn't even know how one got pregnant in the first place, it made the whole world seem dangerous, with sperm lurking on every corner, in every swimming pool, ready to pounce and impregnate.

By the end of my teens and due to the dedicated and enthusiastic tutelage of some hardworking young men, I finally figured out all that sex stuff. I now knew that I couldn't get pregnant because a guy was wearing patent leather shoes. Besides, no guys I knew wore patent leather shoes. Still, I felt much happier knowing I couldn't get pregnant that way, and that no guy was using the reflection in his Converse sneakers to look up my skirt. I was free to move on into my twenties, fearless.

So, why didn't I have children then?

Because my twenties were all about dating, dancing, partying, and drinking; not settling down and propagating the species. I was the clichéd Catholic school girl gone wild. Partying was my job. It's frightening to think what would've happened if I had accidentally gotten pregnant like my pretend-stroller-pushing friend Rhonda. Somewhat like the pioneer women, she gave birth one day and was back in the metaphoric field the next day, partying with her baby in one hand and a Budweiser in the other. But I was also shallow and screwed up and would've been a terrible mother. I consider it a great blessing that I was always so astutely aware of how totally screwed up and unprepared for motherhood I was.

During my thirties, my baby was my career. It sucked from my breast every thought, word, and action of my being. I couldn't have a child. If I had a kid, it wouldn't have been about me anymore and, damn it, I was in show business, a career that needed every bit of my ego, vanity, and self-absorption to focus on *me*. I even have to underline "me" now, to show how important me was to me.

I got married well into my forties. And then it was all about me and my husband. The irony is . . . when I finally was old enough to have the wisdom, stability, and resources to raise a child, I'd stopped producing the eggs to make one.

Once, while shopping at IKEA, my husband noticed me talking to a passing baby. His brow wrinkled compassionately, and he said in his sweet Dutch accent, "Y'know, if you want to have children, we can get some." It was a very loving yet strange way of phrasing it, considering where we were. Like we could just follow the white line to the Kid Department, pick one up, throw it in our big blue shopping bag, and assemble it when we got home.

So, why did I never have kids?

I still don't have a snappy response to that question. I went to a therapist for about a year, and in all our sessions, my time was spent nattering away about my career, relationships, and my phobias of public toilets, men with mustaches, and people drinking from my beverages. Not once did I utter even a sentence, not one little word, in any attempt to unravel the mystery of my having-a-baby code. Looking back, the truth becomes very clear to me: Baby-making just wasn't on my list of fun things to do before I die.

So, I'm the woman who will play with your kids for hours, then be perfectly happy walking away from them and back to "my life." That's enough. I don't need to have any of my own.

And if I ever change my mind, I can always, as my husband suggested, "Get some."

Call Me Peculiar—You Won't Be the First

Suzanne O'Neil

I never wanted kids. I *did* want to get married. I can still picture the limousine and the prospective bridegroom looking with horror at his wristwatch while the best man wipes his brow, and then I walk down the aisle of Holy Name of Mary Church on the arm of my adoring Daddy. I wanted a bridal veil with an enormous train and a frontispiece that would be raised by my cute new husband for our first kiss after God had made us *one*, and there would be at least four bridesmaids looking on, all of us sweltering in scratchy organdy on a June afternoon. I wanted to dance our first dance to "Somewhere My Love" or "Love Theme from *The Godfather*" at the Huntington Town House in Long Island right before we were served our fruit cup on the dais.[1]

But I never wanted kids. I wanted to experience the drama (and attention) of pregnancy—sending my poor husband for pickles and ice cream at three in the morning, bursting into tears as frequently as the character Katie on *My Three Sons*. Just as I hit puberty, Katie Douglas appeared on my cultural horizon and was always bursting into tears about some stupid thing—particularly when the stupid thing made her happy. Then Robbie or Uncle Charlie would mutter, "Women!" I understood this well. I grew up in a houseful of brothers who would remark upon any of my pitiful forays into womanhood, "Look—she's trying to act like a girl!" which they would say in the same tone they'd use if I had been trying to act like Sammy Davis, Jr. So I learned to be as brusque and masculine as I could to escape that scalding humiliation.

Okay, I'll *admit*. Maybe there was a second when I thought of kids. But then I imagine the father of my kid muscling his way into the delivery room and observing what happens to the cellulite on my thighs when they are inverted. He pukes all over me and immediately remembers an urgent appointment in Bangladesh. And even if he is tender—after a few days of getting flowers and candy—the last thing on Earth I'd want is to have to go home and start waiting on a baby: "You mean . . . I have to take that thing *home* with me?"

If I had a daughter, I'd be jealous of her and accuse her of trying to steal her father away from me. If I had a *son*, I'd want him to be not only *gay* but also sufficiently maladjusted to never want to leave home. And there's also the possibility that he might turn out to be Norman Bates.[2]

I know as a mother I would demand that my kids believe in Santa Claus for their entire lives just like I do. If they did not, I would consider them soulless and depraved and kick them out of the house the *moment* they stopped believing. And if they're such smart eight-year-olds, they can take care of themselves.[3]

Eventually, my kids would expect to be entertained. But entertainment has changed a lot. Once upon a time it was the fief of such admirable reprobates as Bugs Bunny, smug, stuttering Babbitts like Porky Pig, and that thwarted hulk of jealousy that was Daffy Duck. They've all been taken over by relentlessly well-meaning vegetables and the tinny optimism of Dora The Explorer, who I wish to god would go explore another galaxy already.

Also, a kid needs to read. I refuse to bring an innocent child into the world who would end up reading *Huckleberry Finn.* I would rather my kid did *not* because it contains racism. The racism it portrays really happened even if we prefer to "pretend" that it did not. (People who don't get Mark Twain have no business associating with children!) And if my kid wanted a toy, as all kids do, personally I want no truck with anyone else's vomit, mucus, feces, flatus, or chicken pox vesicles.

I think the worst thing about having a kid would be that I'd have to share my french fries, something I won't do with my best friend. Actually, I don't eat a lot of french fries these days, since they turn me into a far-too-reasonable facsimile of Charles Laughton, but I'm taking no chances.[4]

Has anyone realized that with each kid they have it makes their feet grow a size larger? This is something my feet do every year all by themselves. This means that if I gave birth to three children, by the time I was forty, I'd be vainly trolling the shoe site Zappos for size 18 Mary Janes. Thank you, but I'm already nicely set up in the varicose-vein department.

Whenever I think of myself as a mother, I see a child in an ill-fitting undershirt and a loaded diaper capering on a denuded front lawn in a trailer park strewn with cheap plastic toys and one door from a 1974 Chevy Chevette. In the kitchen there's an unwashed plastic bowl glistening with the memory of whole milk with one dried Fruit Loop clinging to its side.

My husband is a truck driver with a receding hairline, a shoulder-length ponytail, backne, and an exposed buttock cleft. Our old black-and-white TV has poor vertical control and is always tuned to either Mutual of Omaha's *Wild Kingdom* or reruns of *Flipper*, usually the one that guest-starred Huntz Hall. I weigh 490 pounds, smoke Winstons, and wear muumuus over my shapeless girth. I have four teeth. They're all on the bottom.

Call me peculiar; you won't be the first. I never wanted kids.[5]

My Mother's Final Wishes

Debbie Kasper

In my thirties and forties, people used to ask me, "Why don't you have kids?" I usually got defensive about it, muttering something back like, "I had one, but I forgot where I put it." Then I'd smile feebly. Now that I have become that woman of a certain age—the one where people ask me that same question, but in the final past tense, "How come you *never had* kids?" They ask with such tender despair and incredulity as if it were a mistake, as if I'd forgotten, as if I'd left the house without my pants.

It's too late. I had one egg left, but it was rotten. Even my grocery bag boy knows it's too late for me; even he knows that my last egg dropped and my ovaries are dried-up turkey basters that couldn't conjure up a fertile egg if its whole turkey-baster life depended on it. And even if there were one shriveled-up hard-boiled rotten egg left up in there from the seventies, it would never find a date. No sperm would want it. It would be a dried-up bitter old ovum with a big mouth. It would die alone.

I was always too self-centered and irresponsible to have kids. I know that never stopped many others, but I am a narcissist with a conscience. My boyfriend won't even let me have a dog until I can learn to put the right CDs back in their proper cases. I think that's harsh and unfair because he's got dozens of CDs, but with only one little dog I feel certain I could get it put away where it belonged. I'm not even a very good plant mommy, truthfully; as I reflect, my plants are all thirsty most of the time. I wait until they scream out in terror before I remember to water them. Several have jumped right off my terrace ledge in search of an owner who will love them. I am just not a nurturer. But the real truth is that I never even considered a child. I never played house as a kid. When other neighbors did, I would be the social worker who'd come in and take people's kids away. Not only did I not want kids, but I thought *nobody* should have any.

I remember on my parent's twenty-fifth anniversary I got drunk enough to ask my mother if it would be a mistake if I never had kids. I'd just decided I had to have a career in showbiz—I had even dreamt up the metaphor early on that *my career would be my child.*

"Showbiz is my baby! That's what I shall nurture. I will feed it, burp it, and forgive it when it pees on me. And when I am old it will desert me, just like children do." Little did I know I was a prophet.

The whole family had met in New York City at my parent's favorite restaurant for a celebration of the shock we all shared, that this married couple had not yet killed each other. I was thirty and was already embracing the idea of a career over a family, but I was still doing the two-step with the feminist dance that being a W-O-M-A-N made me capable of having it all. But as someone cleverer than me once said: Even if we did have it all, where would we keep it? Gloria Steinem would later admit that *having it all* was a crock of feminist shit, anyway.

I had waited for the perfect moment at that celebration to ask her the most intimate thing you can ask a mom besides "Do you douche?" Mother sat there surrounded by her husband, whom she openly resented, and her four children, whom she secretly resented, each of us at varying degrees depending on her mood, her week, and her blood-alcohol content. We had robbed her of who she could have been. We were who she would never be. Her children had been born, her life expectations aborted, so now she had imbued me, her only daughter, with all her hope, rooting from the sidelines for me to reach out and be something.

"Debbie, make something of your life. Go! Do! Make your sad old mom proud. I'm rooting for you! R-E-S-P-E-C-T. Sock it to 'em! Burn your bra, dammit!"

I needed to ask her if I could find happiness without procreating. I waited for the boys to engage themselves in some manly geo-political conversation, perhaps about whether James Bond was slipping Ms. Moneypenny the old Oscar Meyer banger. After the appetizer course, I switched seats with a brother, slid up next to her in the booth, and whispered like we were spies invading Panama.

"Mom, if I decided to never have kids of my own, to never experience the joy of motherhood, would I be missing out on something fantastic, something miraculous? Would my life end up empty?"

Her response didn't surprise me. She said "No," but it still stung like a revengeful bee, over and over. She was never cut out to be a mom. What surprised me was the quickness with which she spit out her answer. As if she'd been mulling over this for thirty years. Like a wound-up Pez dispenser waiting for someone to pull back the mouth and out shoots her not-so-cherry-flavored opinions on life.

"Shirl, if I decided to not have kids, would I be missing out on something fab—"

"No!"

Not even a nice "no," but a big overacted "no" fraught with anger, resentment, sadness, and just a touch of dry vermouth.

"Nooooooo! God dammit!"

As if it weren't even a good question. As if I'd asked her if she wanted to go see the Grateful Dead at Madison Square Garden for Mother's Day.

"It's highly overrated. Anybody can have kids. Anybody. You can't even be a cashier at a Piggly-Wiggly without taking a test. You can't fish in a still water pond in Beanfart, Ohio, without a license, but you need neither of those things to have a kid. You don't need permission, you don't need talent, you don't even need a man anymore. But only *you, Debbie,* can chase your dreams. And by the way it hurts like hell. I still hurt from that big-headed little brother of yours."

"You're sure?" I asked feebly, already knowing her response.

"Oh, I'm sure. I'm positive, baby. Just look around."

I looked around. My youngest brother, Joe, the big-headed one, too young to drink, had swizzle sticks hanging out of his ears. Middle-syndrome brother, Robbie, had the table linen hanging out of his nose like a white river of snot, while my oldest brother, Reid, was stoned, grabbing the ass of the waitress, and my father was egging them all on.

"They're wolves in denim," said Mom sadly as she lit another butt to let me know that that was the end of our mother-daughter session for that decade. We'd had longer conversations about what went better with steak: vodka or gin.

She tried, God how she tried, to cradle us in her arms when we cried, to kiss our boo-boos when we were scraped, to sing us to sleep, croaking out "Puff the Magic Dragon," cigarette grasping onto her lower lip for dear life, the ashes spilling down onto our little foreheads like our own personal Lent, until we'd eventually say, "Please don't sing, Mommy." She only had about two notes in her singing range, and they weren't even good ones. "On Top of Ole Smoky," she'd continue.

I remember at a young age when I first heard about mortality, and that one day I was going to die, and everyone I knew was going to die, and I asked her about it. "Mom is it true, are you and Daddy going to die, and I'm going to die, too?"

"Yep. Now go to sleep."

"But what if I die in my sleep tonight?"

"Then Santa will divide up your Christmas presents between your brothers. All right, then. Bye."

She'd say "bye" like we weren't going to see her in the morning.

Mom's thoughts on affection were passed down to her by Scottish parents, who thought affection was like a roast beef. You only had it on holidays, and even then sometimes it would be tough and tasteless, and those were just the breaks. Her hugs were quick and stiff, like being held by a salty surfboard, and her kisses remembered yesterday's cocktail hour. Shirl's idea of soothing a five-year-old was to say, "That's life, babe. Expect nothing, and you'll never be disappointed." A paper cut would have been more comforting.

I once read an article by Dr. Christiane Northrup that stated, "Our bodies and those of our daughters were created by a seamless web of nature and nurture, of biology informed by consciousness that we can trace back to the beginning of time. Thus, every daughter contains her mother and all the women who came before her. The unrealized dreams of our maternal ancestors are part of us." It knocked my socks off, and cleared things up for me. Every picture of every female ancestor in my family album has an angry woman wearing a dowdy floral dress, an ax in one hand and skinned poultry in the other. These photos, faded but still alive, made me happy I didn't procreate. I don't want my daughter to carry around my unfulfilled dreams, and I certainly don't want her to get stuck with my credit card debt.

As my mother lay dying, I was the dutiful daughter at her bedside. I mopped her brow, I held her hand. Before she could slip away, I asked the question again when now it was *really* too late. "Mom, are you sure I should have never had kids?" She winked at me and said, "I might have been wrong about that." And then she slipped away.

Cheese

Ann Slichter

Most of my Facebook friends don't post photos of themselves. They post photos of their kids.

They do this because they love their children. My gut response is, "I got nothing." My equivalent of a newborn in a onesie is a tight close-up of my purse on a chair.

Most hours of the day I'm fine being childless, but holidays can put me over the edge. Every December I have this fantasy of hiring the squarest-looking actors to play my husband and two children. We would sit in front of the Christmas tree, legs crossed, wearing plaid scarves. I would add a burro in the corner eating red tissue paper. Everybody smile: "Cheese." And that would be my holiday card. Might even make it my profile picture.

Besides clicking the LIKE button, there's little I can do to join conversations and stories about preschool and poop and breast-feeding and first steps.

My life is asking the guy breaking down the salad bar at Gelson's if he can wait two seconds while I get more kidney beans. My life is Googling old boyfriends and watching *The Godfather* on AMC at one in the morning. My life is looking at the cover of *Us Weekly* magazine at the checkout counter and feeling a little less-than because I'm not a hottie showing off a baby bump. My life is full of . . . self.

This was never how I imagined it would turn out. While the checker scans my salad, I wonder, *How did I get here? Shit. Was I just napping my way through my twenties and thirties? Did I royally fuck up?* Having a kid was on my mind, but I just thought it would happen on its own. It almost did.

Right before my thirtieth birthday, I practically hit pay dirt.

I had just gotten hired as a writer on my first television show, and I met a guy, Mr. Z. We dated; we fell in love. It wasn't perfect, but it was pretty great. Early on in the relationship, I woke up feeling strange. Not flu strange, the kind of strange where you know, you just know, you're pregnant.

I called one of my best friends. "What am I going to do?" I said. "Do you want to keep the baby?" she asked. "I don't know. I can't make that decision."

"Do you want to have this baby?" she prodded. "I love Mr. Z; I do want a baby. I just don't want a baby at this very moment."

"Tell you what," she said. "Pray and talk to the baby's soul. Tell the baby you love him/her, you want him/her, just not now. Then take a warm bath."

I followed her instructions to the letter.

I never told my boyfriend. Three days later I got my period.

Four months later, my radar went off. It was a small thing. I noticed new sheets with a blue and beige pattern on his bed. Strike that, it was a *big* thing. We had been dating long-distance, and my instinct told me he was seeing someone else. New sheets? Got it.

While he was at work, I took a cab to the airport and headed home. I didn't leave a note; I just left. We got back together briefly. It didn't last. He got new sheets again.

Ten years later, I went to a medium. (I realize half of you probably just put this book down, or skipped to the next essay. In case you're wondering, a medium has the ability—okay, okay, "claims to have the ability" to talk to people on the other side. But, of course, since you're no longer reading this, you didn't hear that.)

So this medium connected with various dead relatives of mine. Then she said, "Ann, there's a little girl here." I don't know any little girls. "Oh," she said, "this little girl tells me she's your daughter." I swallowed. My mouth went dry. "She says you were pregnant with her and told her, 'Not now.' And then the medium proceeded to tell me verbatim exactly what happened ten years previously. "She's growing up on the other side," she told me. "She's with you in spirit."

During my late thirties, still unmarried and childless, I Googled Mr. Z. He's married to "bed sheets chick," and they have kids. I can't help wondering if I missed the brass ring with that soul.

As I bounced from television job to television job, I watched as one by one my friends got married.

I met a really nice guy at one of those weddings and practically begged him to date me. We were an item for three years. My trainer refers to that relationship as a hostage situation. He exaggerates.

At the same time, many of my friends started having babies. I must have gone to nineteen baby showers in two years. A wise friend told me, "Ann, no one enjoys going to baby showers. We just put on our espadrilles and go because that's what we do. We support."

And I did support. With ninja-like focus I honed my shower-guest skills. I got really good at it. Here's a couple of tips for you amateurs out there. One: Stick to the registry, don't go renegade. Even if the Diaper Genie is the only item left. And, two: When the newborn arrives, parents need sustenance. Days after giving birth, my espadrille friend told me she tore the cellophane off a fancy food basket like a Kodiak bear breaking into a Buick full of groceries. Give new parents food, especially the moms.

Back to relationships and babies.

I never imagined being a single parent. I imagined the whole thing was a package deal. Boyfriend, then husband, then house, then baby. At thirty-seven I started getting nervous. Fuuuuck. I'm fucked. I began altering my life math. I erased the house from the equation. I subtracted the husband. It became boyfriend then baby. That might be doable.

I had a few years left to make this pie-in-the-sky dream work. And there was a wonderful man in my life. An amazing person. Off the charts. All I had to do was convince him to be my boyfriend. I felt that was key. Did I mention he wasn't interested in dating me?

Did I give up? No way. I'm no quitter. On his birthday, I sent Mr. I-Wish-You-Loved-Me a hand-picked selection of artisanal wine and cheeses.

After several attempts by the store to deliver it (he wasn't home), I got a call. "Are you sure you gave us his correct phone number? I just hate to see all this aged Gouda and French Pinot go to waste." Even the clerk was wondering what the fuck I was doing. After four days, three messages from the store, and two calls to his work from me, Mr. Awesome finally picked up the cheese basket. Collecting his present was a low priority, and so was I. My friend Ed said it best: "Ann, don't you get it . . . you're the cheese." I got it.

Since this wonderful guy was never going to love me, I figured I better work on loving myself.

I did some serious inner work after hitting my cheese basket bottom. And even with no eligible dude in sight, I still had an unstoppable urge to nurture.

Luckily for me, Hollywood is full of people who need nurturing. It is an entire town filled with adult-sized babies. It's also a town that wears you down. If you don't believe me, then check out the line of people in Los Angeles waiting eight hours to see Amma—otherwise known as "the hugging saint." Amma is from India, and her followers are worldwide. She once hugged 75,000 people in a twenty-three-hour period. With one embrace she can soothe even the darkest cynic.

Everyone needs love and encouragement. I could make a million dollars if I set up a Nurture Shack near the Coffee Bean & Tea Leaf. Even more if it had a drive-thru.

On my fortieth, the phone rang. "Hello, honey! Happy birthday!" It was my father and my stepmother. After a few minutes of small talk, we got down to brass tacks. "We want you to know, if you want to freeze your eggs, we'll pay for it."

After I hung up the phone, I cried, then laughed a little. Hey, why not? Wouldn't hurt to get a little information anyway. I Googled like my life depended on it and called a cutting-edge clinic out of state. Then the real sadness set in. "We'd be irresponsible if we took your eggs at this point. We're not saying you can't get pregnant; we just draw the line at about age thirty-eight." Gulp. Ouch. Where's that damn hugging saint when I need her?

You know who's starting to look really good to me? Guys with kids. Now I have to clarify. I am not drawn to married dudes. Please. I'm talking single dads. The very first thing I look for if I see a handsome dad with salt and pepper hair walking around is the fourth finger on the left hand. Fourth finger left hand, fourth finger left hand. I will crane my neck like a giraffe to see if there's a gold band on that fourth finger. I won't even allow myself to get a good look at the guy's face until I determine his avail.

If there is no ring, I drift into fantasy mode. This almost always takes place at Trader Joe's. My head will start dreaming up my new life with this guy with the naked fourth finger while I'm wheeling down the aisle with packaged salads and seven different varieties of hummus. I study him. Is he nice to his child? Is he listening to the kid? Does he have half- or full-time custody? Is the guy still in love with his first wife? Does he miss her? Did he cheat on her? Is the kid going to like me?

I eat a pita chip as my imagined new beau pulls out of the parking lot of Trader Joe's with his son in the backseat. I head to the regular grocery store for a few more items.

Back at Gelson's in the checkout counter there's that lame *Us Weekly*. I think of all the comparing and wishing and hoping I've done over the years. Famous pregnant women clad in cute outfits are on every cover. Five months pass, I look at the magazines, same gals, this time they're pushing strollers. Six more months go by, and every publication has "How I lost my baby weight," juice fasts, and low-carb eating plans.

Those silly little magazines are designed to make me feel bad. And I fall for that trick every time. According to them, I've failed.

I didn't get the trifecta. I still desire a solid relationship and have a strong need to nurture. And so for the past several years, I've channeled that energy.

I mean, you don't need a boyfriend to be in a relationship with another human being. And I don't have to be a mom to gently nurture.

I have plenty of friends who need lifting up. And their children like my attention. I'm heaping my extra sugar and love in that direction.

The life equation keeps evolving.

Mother to No One

Andrea Carla Michaels

A dozen years ago, when I was approaching forty, my eight-year-old niece Hanna asked me, "Aunt Andrea, are you married?"
I said, "No, are *you* married?!" She seemed alarmed and asked, "Why would I be married?!" and I said to her, "Well, why would *I* be married?"

She folded her arms and said, "You're weird." "Good weird or bad weird?" She grumbled that she hadn't decided yet.

But it was already so clear to her at eight that people were married and had kids, and if you didn't, you were "weird." It's amazing how young those attitudes start.

This "chat" with my niece didn't prepare me for the now-daily shock of being mistaken for someone's mother.

I overheard my other ten-year-old niece Alexa patiently explaining things to her six-year-old brother, who was piecing together family relationships. He asked who I was the mother of. Alexa dramatically turned to Ricky and exclaimed, "Aunt Andrea is the mother to no one."

So suddenly, I'm the weird aunt out in San Francisco, with glasses on my head. (Usually I can't find my glasses, but here they are, on my head. Last week I was looking for them and, not only were they on my head, I had *two* pairs on my head. It gets worse . . . one pair wasn't even mine!)

Yes, I'm the gal with two pairs of glasses on my head, and, yes, by the way, I have cats.

No kids though. I've never actually wanted children, but I don't usually think about what I don't have, nor do I describe myself by others' terms.

Yet, despite my best efforts, I've accidentally become one of those childless women with cats instead who, folks joke, will die alone, my cats having eaten off half my face.

And, the worst of it is, if I had known how much work pets were going to be, I think I might have had kids anyway. At least they grow up and leave.

Plus, as a former world traveler (my old boyfriend used to say I need to constantly meet new people just so I can tell them my "Dating Game" chaperone stories, but that is for another time!) I now have to arrange my life around my "fur babies," as my friend Patrick calls them. Currently I am down to one cat. BlackJack is an all-black semi-feral mini-panther I was sort of talked into.

It was the second time this self-described "dog person" was talked into a cat. At the time I met BlackJack, I already had a lonely Siamese named Koko, whom I had inherited when Helen, the old woman with the cats upstairs, had died.

Helen was the single "cat lady" upstairs, former world traveler, never married, never had kids. I was the twenty-something writer-girl downstairs who used to help her upstairs with her groceries when she'd come back slightly tipsy from the opera and lunch "with the girls," but our relationship didn't extend beyond that.

She had two Siamese who lived to be twenty-one, and they had died within a year of each other. She had then been given a baby Siamese kitten she named Koko, after some cat detective in a book she was reading. Unfortunately, six months later, Helen died. That's when my life changed.

The Animal Control folks came a'knockin' at my door. They were carrying Koko in a box. He was wailing plaintively. (O.J.'s dog has nothing over Koko when it comes to plaintive wailing.)

Would I take this cat? I protested that I loved to travel, didn't want any responsibility, and was a dog person. Plus we weren't even really allowed to have pets in the building by decree of our landlord, the Evil Mr. Fong. (Helen's cats had been grandfathered in.)

The Animal Control folks pleaded that he was a purebred Siamese, worth $200. ("Then I'm sure you'll find him a home right away," I parried.) But he had papers, and they didn't want to take a beauty like him down to the shelter.

Then, having spotted a sucker, they brought out the real guns. "And if you don't take him, we have to put him to sleep," because they could only hold him for three days. "But you have a no-kill policy!" I cried. They explained that was the ASPCA, but when someone has died, they can only hold a cat for three days before putting him to sleep because they know no one is coming to claim him.

"Oh for god's sake," I exclaimed, "I'll find him a home."

I took that box, out came a gorgeous boy with big blue eyes, and within three minutes I was in love, no longer just a "dog person" but now officially a "pet person." Not a cat lady, mind you. But a "woman who has a cat." I thought there was a distinction. Apparently I was wrong.

Fast forward ten years. We were inseparable, and he would literally block the door anytime I tried to leave. And by "blocking the door" I mean throwing himself against the door and actually blocking it. He was a big boy.

Everyone who entered would think of a new euphemism for "humongous."

"Whoa, who is this big boy?" . . . "My, your cat is substantial," etc. All right already, he was fat.

I thought off and on of getting him company because I love to travel, but I did *not* want to be a forty-something single woman with two cats. That's how it starts, you know.

So, cat sitter in place, I began to travel again. There I was in Phoenix at a Scrabble tournament, and there was this tiny stray black cat who was harassing the other three kitties at my hosts' home. They had let him in, and he began sleeping with me and taking showers with me.

Yes, showers. By the end of the week, again I was in love.

So I brought him home. My cat count was all of two, but immediately people started giving me cat cards . . . and cat calendars and cat magnets. Suddenly, I was becoming Helen, the old woman upstairs with two cats.

If I weren't already a cat lady, well-intentioned friends were going to make me into one.

Gentle Koko, sadly, has passed, and BlackJack terrorizes me.

When I return from trips, he attacks and draws blood.

Neighbors will say, "He missed his mama." But BlackJack is not my child. He is closer to an abusive boyfriend. When he claws me, I hear myself making excuses.

"He didn't mean it, it's just that I left him alone. He's not normally like this. I sort of provoked him.

"If you got to know him, you'd know he's sorry and won't do it again," as I try to explain away my bruises and these deeply embedded scratch marks.

Recently I spent two and a half weeks in Australia, rubbing kangaroo bellies and admiring koalas, who are not bears, as I've learned.

It was the longest I'd ever been gone, and I only came back because the cat sitter was turning twenty-one and was off to Vegas to celebrate . . .

The day I came back, BlackJack was wildly excited to see me . . . and then about a half hour later remembered that I had left him and flew across the room, teeth first into my back while I was catching up on email. *Very* scary. He's my bad boy, and I have the scars to prove it.

So now, apparently I'm the cat lady who never had kids. But does that make me a mother?

When you are a woman without kids, who never wanted kids and doesn't see herself as someone who is without anything, it's always jarring when someone assumes I am someone's mother . . . even if that would-be child is only five, or fifteen, or is actually related. If someone asks if one of my nieces is my daughter, I go into shock and think, "How could this be my little girl?" even though I'm quite capable of having had a thirty-year-old by now (or thirty-five-year old, if things had gone really wrong in high school).

I live in a building with only six units. Because of rent control, I will be there till they carry me out or until the Evil Mr. Fong finds a way to kill me.

So little by little, I have become the new "old woman upstairs with cats," even though in my head I'm the twenty-six-year old free spirit who moved in temporarily, because at "any moment, I might move." For years, I didn't even get furniture, thinking I may have to go live with Arcangelo in some town in northern Italy that had no movie theater. (Deal killer, as it turns out!)

But over the years, I've morphed into the quasi manager as a series of twenty-somethings move in and out as they get their first jobs in the "big" city, go back to grad school, move in with a new beau or marry, or yes, even leave to have children. I stay the same, but those around me grow up and move on.

Since I work from home, I've always felt mixed about being the gal with everyone's extra key and the one who signs for packages. I'm the "lady upstairs" they can ask if I have a dust pan or some extra hangers, or something that didn't automatically come with the new neighbor's apartment.

But I'm not their mother. Or am I?

Last year, the twenty-four-year-old boy downstairs invited me to his birthday party. He is in finance (the writers and artists who used to flock to San Francisco can no longer afford an apartment in my rundown building, which is centrally located in a really nice neighborhood, despite my slumlord, the aforementioned Evil Mr. Fong), which meant that his party was going to be mostly "pre" drinking, before he and his buds go out to a real bar to drink. Friday night, 8:00 to midnight.

So I was pleased to be included; I like when the folks in "my" building socialize and look out for one another. I was thinking I'd pop by around ten, give Jonah a little gift, hang out for an hour, and go back upstairs and watch my taped episode of *The Bachelorette* or *America's Next Top Model.*

At ten I go downstairs and enter the apartment teeming with folks I don't know, and the party literally comes to a halt. I mean, if there had been a record playing (you know, the kind on a turntable before it became hip to actually have a turntable again) you could have heard the audible screech/scratch to a halt.

The first twenty-something-year-old "boy" comes up to me, alarmed, and says, "Are we making too much noise?" I smile sweetly and explain I'm the gal upstairs, so they are welcome to make whatever noise they want.

The second one says, "Are you calling the cops?!"

Mind you, it's only ten on a Friday night, and as the reality of who they see me as begins to sink in, I meekly reply, "I was invited."

Jonah however is nowhere in sight to vouch for my inexplicable presence at his shindig.

A third boy comes out of the kitchen zeroing in on me and brightly exclaims, "Hi! Are you Jonah's mother?!" I give up, extend my hand, and say, "Yes I am!" He then says he's heard so much about me.

Mind you, this is San Francisco, and Jonah actually has two mommies . . . so in a matter of five minutes I've been mistaken, variously, for the psychotic neighbor upstairs who would be calling the cops by 10:00 PM on a weekend night, and the lesbian mother of a twenty-four-year old.

I mean, of course, I could be any or all of those things. They don't know me from Adam (Eve?) and are just making assumptions.

But what happened to the assumption that I'm that cool older chick upstairs who is bringing the drugs?

I mean, granted, I'm not . . . I've never so much as smoked a cigarette; I'm a vegetarian who doesn't drink . . . but they don't know that! And damn it, how could I still look so good if I had?!

I wanted to grab him by the scruff of his neck and say, "Listen, young man, there was a time that the party *started* when I entered!" Of course that was never strictly true . . . but still!

I mean, since turning fifty, I have been placed in the role of older woman, someone's mother, lonely cat lady—where "independent and free-spirited," adjectives folks used to ascribe to me, have been daily replaced, "kiddingly" of course, they insist, with "eccentric" and "quirky," and with multiple references to the cats.

Yes, I came to San Francisco thirty years ago to be a hippie (no one told me it had ended fifteen years earlier!), and I still try to live on a barter system and volunteer one day for every day I work for money . . . but when did the daily humiliations begin?

Walking thru the Tenderloin en route to my weekly gig as "Rice Lady" at Curry Without Worry, a fairly well-dressed crack dealer (?) shouts out at me as I'm passing, asking if I have a cigarette. I say no and keep going. He then follows me and says, "'Scuse me, 'scuse me, no disrespect, but I'm really into older women. Are you married?" I lie and say, "I'm taken," as I quicken my pace and keep going.

But then I get to the corner and stop dead in my tracks. I turn around and march back up to him and ask, "How old are you?" "Thirty-one." Oh. "And how old did you think I was?" He says, "I don't know, forties? But if you're in your fifties, that's cool, that's cool."

So, yes, I would be an older woman to him, but I'm irritated at that point and ask if that line "No disrespect but I'm into older women" usually works for him. I mean, granted the two other women he already had with him had no teeth, but really, is that the best pick-up line he has? And am I just a random older woman who looks like I'm looking for someone?

My bad, probably karma, because I used to exclusively date men half my age who didn't speak English.

It should have stopped with Nikolai, who once mentioned his mother was forty-one. I expressed surprise (I thought he was older than twenty-one, he thought I was younger than forty-two) and told him I was older than his mom. He casually surveyed me with his gorgeous, dark, long-lashed Bulgarian eyes and purred, "Yeah, but you don't look like my mama." Ha! Love those foreign boys!

You see, back then, I was nobody's mama, and I was pleased.

So on I continued, and I got away with it till I was about forty-five. The word "cougar" had not yet worked its way into the language, nor was there a television show starring Courtney Cox, who just a few years before was still a twenty-something "Friend."

One day, apropos of nothing, my latest boy toy, Giovanni, says, "I wish I had met you ten years ago." I laughed and said, "But, Giovanni, you would have only been sixteen." "Yes," he continued, "but you must have been really something."

Snap. (If this were live, you would hear a snap of fingers and me being snapped back to reality.)

And voilà, ouch, I was cured.

On my latest trip I went to Australia, in hopes of rubbing a kangaroo belly.

My host was eight-months' pregnant and working on her dissertation. So I was pretty much left to my own devices, traveling about Brisbane on my own.

First day, on a bus to a koala preserve, I struck up a conversation with two young French guys who were also, if my eavesdropping served me right, en route there.

In the old days, I'd have been invited to join them . . . maybe end up traveling with them for the next few weeks, perhaps sleeping with one of them. Now I meekly asked if I could join them . . . trying not to appear too stalkerish/lonely. They were polite about the whole thing and said it would be a pleasure.

When we got to the exceedingly expensive preserve ($33 to walk in, another $17 if we wanted to hold a koala and have our picture taken!)

I joked maybe they could pretend to be my sons and we could go in on a family rate.

Much to my horror, they responded they had just been thinking the same thing! And the worst part was, we weren't even eligible, as "family" meant adults with kids under sixteen.

Alas. Here I was, finally ready to embrace motherhood (to save a couple of Aussie bucks and to enjoy a couple of young French bucks) . . . but no-go.

So, lesson learned? Even if I don't have kids, never wanted kids, or wouldn't have minded having kids, as "*une femme d'un certain age*" I am going to be mistaken for everybody's mother anyway. So I might as well embrace it . . .

Now, come here, sweetie, you have a little schmutz on your face.

Motherhood Adoption Ambivalence

Jeanne Dorsey

For many women there is an ambivalence scale when it comes to motherhood. One wonders how Torry Ann Hansen placed on that scale when she decided to adopt her son from Russia, whom she later returned amid great controversy. In the ideal world, motherhood would be a choice. I'm not talking about abortion and a "woman's right to choose." I'm talking about a woman choosing to be a mother, either natural or, if this is not available to her, adoptive. Along with this choice comes ambivalence. The scale of a woman's ambivalence is for her to assess before deciding to launch into motherhood. I've yet to meet a woman who didn't score at least a .5 on a scale of 10. Of course there are many practical factors that hover around what should be, at its core, a very personal and deeply felt decision. Each of these factors can either raise or lower a woman's level of ambivalence. Will she be raising the child with a partner? Does she think her partner will be equally committed to child-rearing? Will she put a career on hold? If so, will this make her resentful? If not, does she have the sort of job that allows for flexibility while raising a child? Is there enough money? Is there enough family and community support? And if none of these practical factors is stable, is she infinitely patient and good-hearted? Has it always been something she's fantasized about? If she scores upwards of 7 on the ambivalence scale, perhaps she will want to do some serious soul searching. If she scores a 10, perhaps she will decide to pass on the whole experience. In the ideal world, she will be at peace with this choice, and her identity as a woman remains complete. In the real world the stigma of being a childless woman is part of the collective unconscious.

Could the collective unconscious have played even the slightest role in Torry Ann Hansen's need to press on with such an exhaustive procedure as international adoption only to abruptly and tragically recoil when the circumstances proved beyond her control? Who knows what went into her decision to follow through on something that, even a small amount of research will show, is far from a safe bet. Raising one's natural child is a journey into the unknown. To adopt a child under a set of circumstances that are most likely unpleasant is a bold step, requiring much more than the willingness to love a child. Did she feel that little Artyom would complete her identity?

A friend of mine recently completed in vitro treatment and learned she was unable to conceive. When I offered my condolences, she confided in me, "The truth is, I'm not sure I'm cut out to be a mother, but at least I can say I tried. This way, when anybody asks, I can be an object of pity rather than scorn." Sadly, those expressing the thinly veiled scorn tend to be other women.

Several years ago, still single and approaching forty, I mentioned to my then therapist how in our next session I wanted to discuss something that was beginning to dawn on me. Most likely I would never have children. "Yes," she replied, "we do need to talk about that because it's definitely a loss." Feeling no sense of loss, I sent her a brief note in which I thanked her for our work together and informed her that I would no longer need her services. Aren't therapists supposed to support rather than judge as one attempts to come to terms with life's big questions? Ironically I learned that a colleague of mine was this woman's daughter. The daughter, a writer, often wrote about her mother, depicting her as profoundly frustrated in the motherhood role and openly hostile toward her own daughter. Big surprise! I was both amused and saddened by this odd window into the personal life of my lame ex-therapist. Yes, she projected onto me her own ambivalence. But I found this particular psychological cliché to be especially disappointing.

Okay, a run-in with a clumsy therapist, it happens. They're human, after all. But in truth, I was vulnerable to this comment regardless of its coming from a misguided woman's empty mother vanity. Its clumsiness collided with my ambivalence about the huge question of motherhood. At that moment, it felt like society's view rather than an ill-timed comment from one insensitive self-absorbed therapist. In some way, I had failed.

For several years I taught creative writing workshops in public schools throughout New York's five boroughs. Often I worked with special-needs students, many of whom were in the foster system and brought much emotional baggage with them to the classroom. Yet it was frequently the most difficult of these children who responded the most fully to the writing assignments. They had so much to say and a deep desire to be heard. It was during this period when I entertained an adoption fantasy. After all, I had reached some really problematic kids and got them to open up and achieve work that made them feel proud. Surely I could offer a good life to Kervins, or Dahlia, or Jasper. But then I would show up the next week and Kervins would spend the entire class snoring, Dahlia would tell me I was a dumb bitch, and Jasper would say, "Thank you Miss Whatchamacallit, but I'm not in the mood to write poetry today. You can take your crap and go." And I would be roused from my naive dream. On the ambivalence scale, I began to register a solid 10.

One of my closest friends is the proud mother of a gifted fourteen-year-old boy. He is also my friend not because he's the son of someone I'm fond of but because he's good company all on his own; he's preternaturally intelligent, funny, thoughtful, and sociable. She has devoted a large portion of her life to him and at times she admits to feeling the sacrifice, but by and large she is grateful. When I say she is proud, I mean she feels genuinely rewarded by her experience as his mother and takes very little of the credit for what a swell kid he is. "I'm lucky. He's just a nice boy, and really smart, and I don't know how much I have to do with any of it." It's a comfort to witness my friend participate in what I view as one of life's grand experiments and end up with this experience.

It is not an experiment in which I will have the chance to participate. Motherhood is not in the cards for me. Is it a loss? How would I know? I'm too busy living. I am blessed with a full, healthy, and interesting life. And then every once in a while, true to my gender, I ask myself: How would I feel if I were someone's mother? And how would that someone feel about me? I will never know. "There is nothing either good or bad but thinking makes it so."

The Flying None

Tracy Smith

L ast summer, I made a pilgrimage to the remote north of Ontario, Canada, to spend some time chatting with my beloved Aunt Margaret. Margaret is spending her final years in a nursing home for Catholic nuns so, suffice it to say, I did not make this trip for the promise of being remembered in a will. I made this trip because I love her and always leave her presence with something valuable to take away: a sense of self-worth, and, as always, another set of plastic prayer beads. I think that nuns keep prayer beads in a drawer like dentists keep new toothbrushes. Makes me wonder: If I kept a set of prayer beads for too long as I do toothbrushes, would they get all germy from my sins? What if a guy spent the night at my house and I told him there were some fresh prayer beads in the medicine cabinet—would he think I was a harlot for being so prepared?

Once Margaret had given me a pamphlet (nuns also always have pamphlets) about the "vocation" of being a single woman with no children. She said that the single life, which I had not yet considered pitiable, could be seen as just as much of a calling as being a nun had been for her. I had laughed the whole thing off, wondering how on Earth a menopausal Catholic nun could possibly draw any parallels between herself and me, a twenty-seven-year-old, nearly atheist, stand-up comic with great boobs and plenty of eggs left in the basket. Was I really more like her than I was like my five sisters with children? Let's consider them one by one.

My sister Bonnie kicked things off at age eighteen. She married, had two kids, and had her tubes tied by age twenty-one. Some people will do anything to get away from home and also avoid taking the SATs. Trudy compared getting her husband locked into domesticity to the act of trapping a squirrel with bread crumbs leading to a crate. She had four kids and seemed to live only to send us the perfect Christmas card with all of them in matching outfits. Colleen moved to Vancouver, British Columbia, a city where the female-to-male ratio was 5:1 and a gal had to be pretty impressive to catch a man. So, while going to the great lengths to impress, Colleen was paralyzed in a parachuting accident. But this "minor setback" of not being able to walk did not quiet her call to motherhood. Eventually, Colleen quit taking birth control and allowed her fascinating self to be impregnated by an unhappily married man. She would sooner be a paraplegic single mom than go through life childless. Bernadine married her true soul mate in that she and her husband both loved to drink at beach bars in Florida without a care in the world. Still, her call to motherhood was louder than a bar full of drunks singing "Margaritaville," so Bernadine had a son. And just when someone might have suggested she get a job, she had another son. It's funny how people who love to drink always have some kind of problem with breast-feeding. He won't latch on. Maybe he just doesn't feel like having a drink that early in the day. Maureen, the baby of the bunch, out-mothered us all by marrying at twenty-one and commencing to drop one baby after another until there were five. The only saving grace of that lot in life is that she has no sense of smell and is unaffected by the odor of a crap-filled diaper. I once spent an entire weekend trying to put a dent in the laundry at Maureen's house, and my ovaries tied themselves in a knot. I also found myself saying things that single girls never say, like "Stop licking that!"

According to my Aunt Margaret, I wasn't just a woman who had not mastered the art of trapping a mate in my love nest or stealing fertilizer or getting out of one dreaded task for what seems to be the super cushy life of a stay-at-home mom; I had a calling from God. I had a "vocation." I wasn't just a crass and stubborn unmarriable misfit—I'd been given these "gifts" from Heaven above to be a source of strength and inspiration, a light that would descend into the homes and lives of my sisters now tethered to one place by their burdens in motherhood. I had a call to the servitude of my ever-expanding flock. (Even if this were my belief, I would have had to keep it under wraps. Any such notions of my feeling that saintly would undoubtedly turn my sisters into a torch-carrying mob ready to take me down a few pegs and stomp the light out of my halo.)

At age twenty-seven it seemed to me a little soon to kneel down and be anointed into such a commitment. I still had plenty of fertile years ahead of me and was not about to accept being pacified by the notion of substituting the words "chosen one" for "childless spinster." Even Jesus spent a little time wandering in the desert before getting to the business of being a messiah. So I went on doing comedy on the road (just like Jesus), flying from city to city making people laugh until there I was, twenty years later, fanning myself in a room everyone else thought was cold.

As of today, I have sixteen nieces and nephews and seven great nieces and nephews. Without my own absolutely perfect children to compare and compete with, I can bring the extra love sometimes needed by the ones who feel disenfranchised. I've brought guitars and stand-up comedy recordings, tales of adventure and travel, and, dare I say, inspiration. I don't have any pamphlets or prayer beads, but I always have a good book to suggest, and I know that if you read a good book at an Irish pub, you will always end up talking to someone smart. My older nieces and nephews have friended me on Facebook. They confide in me and at least act like they think I know what I'm talking about. They make promises to visit me—if and when I ever stay put.

Last summer, when I made that trip to see Aunt Margaret, I accepted her gift. I was one of many visitors Aunt Margaret has all of the time. I accepted my "vocation" of being the single and childless one among a group who would need the blessings and bounty of my freedom. I am a peripatetic nucleus, and part of each of the families branched from my own parents. And far contrary to the fears portrayed in the Bridget Jones diaries or any other female-authored book with a martini glass or a stiletto heel on the cover, I will not die alone.

POSTSCRIPT: If you've noticed a math error in the number of nieces and nephews I have, it's because I also have three brothers not mentioned in this story. My mother was a saint.

Not's Landing

Beth Lapides

L ately, because I gave up the booze, I'm really getting how much energy it takes to *not* do something. And how much of not doing things I've done and sometimes not done. Not eating. Not smoking. Not sexing. Not becoming my mother. Not *not* becoming my mother. Not obsessing. Not being afraid. Not writing. Not having a real job. Not giving in to time. And, most pertinently here, not having kids.

Not having kids is saying one big no. No to the same thing over and over and over. So that you can say yes to everything else. Having kids is saying one big yes so that you can say a million little nos in the hopes that you might end up with a child who is alive and has a good conscience and boundaries and plan for living without being too afraid.

I picked one big no and a million little yeses. I didn't want to have to say no all the time. I'm already such a negative person. Cheerful, but negative.

If you don't believe me, maybe you will believe Greg. Greg is the man I didn't have children with. Some women meet a man and think *This is the father of my children.* I met Greg and thought, *Now here's a man I cannot have kids with.*

We married, but I never liked calling him my husband. In fact I spent a lot of time *not* calling him "my husband." I found it annoying that the words *husband* and *wife* refer etymologically to ownership and emotionally to a particular kind of relationship that most often involves having kids.

"You're so negative for a positive person," he once said. "No, I'm not!"

I thought about having kids, of course. But why do today what you can put off forever?

On a gut level, I just didn't want to have kids. I thought maybe I should anyway. In fact, maybe I should *especially* because I didn't want to. Like the way you should exercise especially when you feel lazy. Reach out and connect especially when you feel isolated. Share especially when you feel greedy. But having kids especially because I didn't want to? It didn't seem like bringing another person onto the Earth as a contrary action to my character flaws of selfishness and fear seemed wise. Or fair to the kid.

Not to mention that it seemed unfair to everyone else already on Earth. Even as a teenager I was very taken with the idea that over-population was the root cause of every other problem on Earth. (I'm sorry, Senator Kennedy, but what about just less offspring?) And I felt that if you didn't *have* to have kids maybe just do something else.

Plus, I just didn't *want* to.

I didn't want to from the time I was fifteen. I was in the passenger seat of my not-smart-enough boyfriend's jacked-up blue Nova, headed to my ancestral family tract home, fantasizing about escaping into my real life. The boyfriend threw some trash out the window. I huffed about his littering. And then I had a thought. *I'm never going to have kids. You can't do everything, and I'm an artist and I'm going to do that and not have kids.* I didn't say anything because he wasn't the one who I was going to not have kids with. I knew that much. I resolved it so strongly that until now, writing this piece, it never occurred to me that I might be living a grown-up life designed by a fifteen-year-old. I was a very strong-willed fifteen-year-old. So strong willed that that version of me still sometimes bosses this version of me around.

Because maybe that was just a rationalization. As a grown-up, I've met plenty of women who have had careers they loved and also had kids. But I've also met plenty who've made too many compromises. Plenty of guys who have done the same. I had no dreams of family life. I had a dream of an art life. If there had been enough money, I think I would have liked to have a child along for the ride.

Then there was the pain. Pain is something I have definitely tried to not have. But you know what they say: No pain, no life.

Somewhere right around the time I was thinking maybe I was wrong about not having kids, a yoga teacher did an adjustment on me. After the adjustment, the sound of ripping.

"Is that your pants?" he asked, adding insult to injury.

In the following months, I tried to heal the hamstring with every combination of heat and ice I could think of, including whiskey on the rocks. Finally the teacher sent me to see Mimi and Moses Yu. A husband-and-wife team of acupuncturists who ran a low-rent clinic in East L.A. The luck of the draw assigned me to Mimi. She had me pull down my pants and lie on the table. It didn't not hurt. It didn't not hurt so much I started to cry.

"You can't take the pain," she said. "Jewish girls so spoiled. You better never have baby." Is that even legal to say?

Then she twiddled the needles in her own neck, in the Frankenstein spot, to prove she could take the pain.

Over the course of eight treatments, the injury was healed. Like fire, sometimes you can fight pain with pain. You don't notice the absence of pain until there is pain. In the same way, you don't notice the absence of children until there are children. I like children by the way. It was never that. And they like me. Liking has nothing to do with it.

Mimi Yu reminded me of my mother, who also once told me she didn't think I should have children. They are both tough, no nonsense, straightforward, partner coupled. Every now and then, the more sensitive Moses Yu would come in and twiddle my needles. He had such a light touch. I wished the universe had assigned me to him. But then again, Mimi healed the pain. And told me to stop thinking so much and go home and watch some "stupid TV."

Because Mimi Yu told me I shouldn't have a baby, I started thinking about having a baby.

All my yoganini girlfriends were doing natural childbirth on sheepskin-covered beds or in tubs of water, orgasming and going inside the pain. I started to want to experience childbirth. Just so I could prove that I could take the pain. I *couldn't* really take the pain though. That was one of the reasons for all that booze.

I started thinking maybe there was a way to not have a kid but not not have a kid. Had no idea what that would be.

Then came the last night of a five-day visit from my parents. We were sitting around the living room of our Los Feliz apartment trying to think of something to talk about. We'd covered everything. We should have been watching TV, but my parents felt they didn't see me nearly enough and wanted to squeeze in every last second of chatting.

"What else?" my Dad asked.

There was nothing else.

"Well," said Greg, "we're thinking of donating sperm to this lesbian couple."

I motioned across my throat the universal sign for *cut*. Stop talking! And he did stop. But so what? It was too late. The baby was out of the birth canal.

My dad started to hyperventilate, unloosened his belt, and hoisted himself out of our thrift store chic gold velvet armchair. It swiveled. My head spun. My mom turned the little wheel on her yellow Bic lighter and took a big drag off her Pall Mall.

"No," she said on the exhale.

Of course no wasn't for her to say in this case.

And I was loving the idea. It would be like we had kids without having kids. I would be like an aunt, but more. Or less. There would be this child on Earth that I'd be connected to in this special way. But she'd, or he'd, already have two moms, plus Greg as a something. I liked the whole weird feel of it. A mom but not a mom. Responsible but not responsible. Helpful but not smothering.

"Greg will be connected to these women in a way that doesn't involve you," she said panicking. That didn't bother me at all.

My dad came back in with a few thumbs of scotch in his tumbler.

"You know," he said, "you're grown up now. And you don't have to tell us everything. And in the future, nothing about sperm."

Way to draw a boundary, Dad! I was excited. We needed more boundaries in my family. This was a good start. The fact that my parents do want me to share everything is part of the claustrophobia of family life that was another thing that kept me from wanting to have kids.

Maybe that's one reason people have kids. To give them something to talk to their parents about that's not them. It's like a privacy hedge.

As it turned out, that particular lesbian couple decided not to procreate. And so we never did expand our family that way. Soon after that, another friend, single and desperate to have kids, said, "Well, if nothing else works, I can always borrow your husband's sperm." Like it was sugar or something. Yes sure, bring over the measuring cup. That never happened either.

But here's what did happen: I manifested a daughter. It was a miracle. Even my own negativity could not get in the way.

I'd always said I'd have a daughter if I could have an eighteen-year-old. Ha ha.

And then one day the phone rang.

"Do you ever have interns?" asked a sweet girl on the other end. We never had, but we could. She said she came to our show, The Un-Cabaret, quite frequently, and really loved it. So she was smart enough to open with flattery. I liked that. So I said come over. We sent her on a Xeroxing run, and she did a good job. I asked if she was hungry. She looked hungry.

"Yes, I'm always hungry," she said. So I made her some chili. And that was that.

I got to be a mother to an eighteen-year-old. Not a mother mother. Not a stepmother. Not a surrogate mother. Not a foster mother. But what I came to think of as a pseudo mother.

Her name is Jaime. Like *J'aime*. I love.

I got to be a pseudo mother without tapping into my deep well of negativity. Yes, she could drop out of college for which she was accruing debt to major in a field she was only studying to please her parents who weren't paying for it. I got to tell her yes she could work for my radio show. I got to tell her yes it was okay to start having sex. I got to tell her yes she should try to become a location scout. And yes to becoming a teamster. And yes to quitting her job so that she could go back to school for pre-med and yes to med school as an older student. And then one day, she was driving away in a new car that her on-again, off-again, big-time screenwriting boyfriend had given her.

I hired her, I encouraged her, I fed her, I gave her clothes. Now I only see her on Facebook. And maybe I will hardly ever get to see her again. But I love her. I love her in that way that isn't a friend or a lover or anything besides a child. Even though she's not mine. And maybe for me that was the most important part of not having a child. Learning to love and not want to possess. To put away no and start saying yes.

Sitting on the Fence

Maureen Langan

An 800 number on the side of the home pregnancy box said to call if you had any questions.

"Hello," a soothing voice answered.

"Are you the 1-800-pregnancy Lady on the Box?" I asked.

"I'm a registered nurse who works for the company. How can I help you?"

"I realize you're a nurse, not a therapist. I never met a therapist who works on the side of a box. Then again, I never met a nurse who did either. Until you. The point is, I'm scared. Terrified. Out of my mind. I've never been pregnant before, and I'm forty-one.

"I don't feel lucky. I feel scared. I have commitment issues. That's why it took me so long to get married. I grew up in an alcoholic family. I was the *parentified* child. Do you know what that is? Well, you wouldn't think a parentified child would be afraid to parent, but I am . . . because . . .

"Yes, I do have a doctor. And a therapist.

"Yes, I understand you just answer questions about the pregnancy test."

When I hung up I was still scared out of my mind. I soon learned there was nothing to be afraid of—six weeks later I had my first miscarriage.

I knew I was on the fence about having children when I had a miscarriage and my response was "Whew! That was close." Actually, I've had six. If comedy comes in threes, then six miscarriages must be twice as funny.

The truth behind that joke is that there was relief in my miscarriages, but there was also sadness. I was trying to get pregnant, but not necessarily because I wanted to. The song "It's Now or Never" played on a loop in my head. Do I really want a baby? If I don't have one now, I'll never have one. I'll never run the turkey trot with my daughter on Thanksgiving morning. I won't applaud my son when he stands up to the school bully. I'll never be a "mom." There is a sadness in realizing that. Remember high school? Getting invited to the party was what mattered, whether you wanted to go or not. Being pregnant, even for a short time, made me feel invited to a party that I wasn't sure I wanted to attend. "But everyone's going . . ." That's a powerful mind fuck. And I got pregnant so easily at my age that I thought maybe it was meant to be. These thoughts were a motivator, but not a feeling changer. If I had ten more years of fertility, I would have put off trying for ten more years. Each time the pregnancy didn't take—despite my husband's crossed fingers behind his back as the doctor shared another lifeless sonogram—I felt sad, but my sadness did not dissuade my relief.

Calling the 800 Lady on the Box was reactive. I had a sense of urgency, a need to quell my fear. Like a man calling a sex line, it was anonymous, immediate, and satisfying for the moment. I could tell the Lady on the Box my innermost fears and, even if she judged me, she was only on a box.

I can't give you one simple clear-cut reason as to why I was so frightened. There's never been a moment of clarity when I said, "No kids for me." In fact, it's been the opposite. As the oldest girl in a family of six children, I thought one day I'd have a child. One day. Just not today.

I have ten nieces and nephews I can't stop hugging and loving. I talk to children on the street and say, "How wonderful, chocolate sprinkles on rainbow sherbet, I wouldn't have thought of that. You must be brilliant." "I am," the little boy answers.

A brown-skinned girl walks out of the gym after a swim class on a cold winter day. She's swaddled in a parka with a white fur-trimmed hood around her sweet little face. I ask her if she's an Eskimo. "No," she answers proudly, "I'm a guppy."

An obituary in *The New York Times* read, "Mrs. Farthingpucker had no children. She bequeathed all her assets to the ASPCA." It made me sad. I didn't want to be her or the Schaffers. The Schaffers were the older couple who lived around the block. "Poor things were never able to have children of their own," the neighbors whispered. I envisioned my obit as reading: "Maureen was surrounded by her adoring, devoted, brilliant children who can't stop sobbing over the loss of their most precious gem."

At forty-one, I decided to try to get pregnant—kind of like knocking on the door when you know no one's home. Surprisingly, I got pregnant easily. I had five pregnancies in three years, but I never got out of the first trimester. I agreed to try in-vitro fertilization once at a cost that should only make you angry. The drugs arrived in a Styrofoam cooler. That cooler stayed in the refrigerator for three months before I lifted the lid. I would have been more excited had the cooler contained a Lobster Gram.

I wanted to say "Yes" to a child like that show *Say Yes to the Dress*. Everyone tells the bride how perfect the dress is, but she knows it's not right for her. No matter how many mirrors she looks in or from what angle, it just doesn't seem right. Whenever I tried on "child," it felt too tight, too constricting. I couldn't breathe.

Lord knows I tried to have children. I've had five natural pregnancies and one IVF. That's trying, isn't it? It is. Of course it is. But what woman waits until she's forty-one to start conceiving if she really wants kids? Who was I fooling?

I was a passive player in my procreation; I let my actions, or lack thereof, make the decision for me. When I was thirty-seven, my doctor told me my fertility was fading fast, to screw or get off the bed. Still, I put off trying for another year, then another, then two more. I let God or my biology or destiny make the decision for me. I'd say things like, "If it's meant to be, it'll be." By not making a decision, and putting it off, I made a decision.

I hurt for women and men who want children more than anything in life. But no matter what you ask for or plan for, life doesn't always respond kindly.

I think of the playwright Wendy Wasserstein, who gave birth to a daughter at the age of forty-eight. Six years later, she died of cancer. Was it the in-vitro drugs in her system that caused the cancer? Who knows?

I saw an elderly couple at Kennedy Airport pushing their grown son in his wheelchair, his lifeless arms at his side, his head drooping, his parents worn out.

Both Wendy and that older couple made me think: If I have a kid in my 'forties, will she be healthy? Will I live long enough to care for her? I asked the doctor's assistant what my chances were of having a child with Down syndrome. With her gum-snapping attitude she responded, "No you didn't! Don't you know that saying things can make them happen?" If that were true, Wendy would still be here and that elderly couple's son would be out of a wheelchair. My brother's brain would be okay, my father wouldn't drink, and my fears would be gone. Saying things doesn't make them happen.

If I were on a game show hosted by the deceased Richard Dawson and he said, "Pick a word that instantly comes to mind when I say 'child.'" I would respond, "Trapped. Richard, I pick 'trapped'—enormously, overwhelmingly, throat-constrictingly trapped." Even if he didn't ask, I'd say the second word would be "family."

I grew up in a family, and I didn't like it very much. Parts of it were fine, but overall I wouldn't call it a pleasant experience. Family to me meant alcohol and anger and fear. It was *Long Day's Journey into Night* over and over again.

There were happy times, like riding my youngest brother, Michael, on the front of my banana-seat bike into town to get twenty-five-cent ice cream cones at the Kozy Diner. We'd come home to our mother in the kitchen hovering over a sink full of dishes, whistling. Hers was not a happy whistle, but rather the long, lingering whistle of anger and disappointment, whistling as she slammed another soapy dish into the drain board.

My father was funny. Sometimes. He ate ice cream with me and watched *It's a Mad, Mad, Mad, Mad, World*. He told me I would go far in life because I had moxie like Eydie Gorme. He often came home with red eyes. Standing just feet away from him, I could smell if he'd had three or six beers, if he had them that day or the night before. Beer has an odor that comes through the pores. Old beer in a body is a smell that makes me recoil. "Tell them he's sick in bed," my mother would say when the New York City Sanitation Department called. We weren't allowed to tell our friends what dad did for a living. We told them he drove a truck; we just didn't say it was a garbage truck.

I also wasn't allowed to tell my friends that my brother Hugh had brain damage. "It's no one's damn business," my mother said. Hugh didn't look brain damaged, and he was very sweet when he wasn't having a fit. I was ten when Mom explained to me that Hugh's brain was slightly injured, the result of the measles when he was a toddler. She said the technical term was "neurologically impaired."

Hugh was ten and a half months and one day older than me. When the kids at Knollwood Elementary School singled him out for being odd, taunting him with chants of "Hughie, Hughie, Hughie," I wanted to trip them, and as they were falling face first onto the asphalt, I'd calmly say, "No. He's not weird. Technically, he's neurologically impaired." Instead, I told them to shut up and walked away wishing he were different.

"Have a child. It forces you to put another's needs before your own. You clean up their spills, you deal with their tantrums." How often have I heard that? I didn't need a kid to learn those lessons.

At night I'd sit at the top of the stairs outside my bedroom listening to my father calling my mother names that men aren't supposed to call their wives as another coffee mug shattered against the living room wall, my mother slashing back, "You're useless."

Sitting on those stairs, I felt trapped, my throat constricting, and fear flooding my body. I'd think crazy thoughts, like what happens if I accidentally swallow my tongue? My father said a man on his job swallowed his tongue and died. Some nights I'd sleep on my stomach with my head dangling over the side of my bed, hoping the gravity would keep my tongue to the front of my mouth, far away from my throat, and me alive for another day.

I was fifteen years old and a freshman in high school when my sister Anne, the youngest, was born. She was a beautiful respite from the whistling, and fighting, and fear. I was chosen to be her godmother.

I was delighted when the women at Foodtown stopped to ask if the red-cheeked child in the cart were mine. In many ways she was. I'd bring her to college with me, where she'd sit in the back row drawing pictures. We read *The Importance of Being Ernest*. When she was in grade school, I reassured her she was not gay just because she didn't like the boys in her class and never would. I bought her a fancy bra and dress at Sears for her eighth grade dance. At the beach, I insisted she call me Aunt Maureen when cute guys were around. "Mo" was one letter away from "mom," and I didn't want any deterrents. I was her maid of honor when she got married, and I was on the phone with her while she was in labor about to give birth to her first child.

I may not be anyone's official mother, but I have done a lot of mothering in my life. I was more of a mother when I should have been more of a child. I don't resent it. Life isn't always linear or chronological. In fact, I'm glad I got to experience that mothering energy. It's a part of me. It always will be. It's why I can be okay with not having children because I have nurtured. But now, as an adult, it's my time to experience a more carefree life. It may not be the typical order of life, but it's the order of my life.

Today, I am an adult with the freedom to travel the world, eat whatever I want, host a radio show, bike the Portola Valley, hike the coast of Ireland, run with Maxie, my Wheaten Terrier. I open my front door, not to fear, but to possibilities. I don't feel trapped.

And when my mother says to me in her Irish brogue, "You're always somewhere hopping, jumping, and skipping." Yes I am. Better late than never. One thing is for sure—I won't be whistling as I chuck dishes into a drain board.

You'll Never Babysit in This Town (Again)

Suzy Soro

I like peace and quiet. Relaxing at a cemetery on the beach is my idea of a perfect vacation. The last time I left town, I flew first class (coach), and as the plane lifted gently into the air, the child sitting next to me emitted such a piercing scream we lost cabin pressure. It made me miss the smokers; at least a cigarette goes out in three minutes. A volume-control function available on any small model of child ages two through seven would be a plus for humanity.

I'm a standard loner, the kind that neighbors talk to the press about after we've committed a horrible crime. My crime? Not having kids, because I never wanted children.

I believe this is a perfectly acceptable reason, but to some people (Mom) it isn't good enough. For some women (Aunt Helen), this implies there's something wrong with me, like I'm not a real woman because a real woman wants children. Oh, to find that in writing somewhere . . .

When your family crest is four people clutching dead memories and daring the others to let go first, finding room for a child on that coat of arms requires adult-sized thinking. At nineteen, numerically an adult, I dated a boy I almost married (close call), and I seriously thought about having a child. But I also seriously considered buying stone-washed jeans. Obviously, nineteen is not a good age for making major fashion choices, not to mention bringing someone into your life who will then mock those choices when they hit puberty.

I know I wouldn't make a good parent. My apartment isn't child-proofed, and I have ghosts in my closet. The bogeyman lives under my bed. And if talking to mothers on the phone is any indication, you apparently have to hang up when your child is bleeding (rude). Now, I wouldn't have known that. When a friend's five-year-old I was babysitting said, "I'm going to drink a gallon of SunnyD in under a minute," I pulled out a stopwatch. It made sense to me. I did reckless, crazy things as a child. Like talk to strangers (my father). How would I know enough to keep my kid from doing reckless, crazy things? Is letting a little kid drink a gallon of fluid in under a minute reckless and crazy? I thought it was just good old-fashioned fun (voyeurism).

I'm not in the best of shape. I'm also incredibly lazy. And kids move around a lot, and not to the market to buy you vegetables (candy). They need to be watched, supervised. And since I now spend more time on YouTube than I spent in high school, I don't think I'd be right for that job. I also need to control every aspect of my life, which leaves no room for spilled milk or a skinned knee. Who has time for a mani-pedi with all that milk and blood to mop up? And children are always in some stage of stickiness. This is fine if you want to use them as a bulletin board or to seal packages, but I admit to more than a touch of OCD. I've scrubbed my French side tables so many times I can see the fingerprints of the carpenter who built them in 1879. If I did this to a kid, I'd be left with one very sticky, bleeding skeleton.

When I was young, I asked my parents so many questions they routinely answered, "I don't know," which led me to conclude they were idiots. Is idiocy genetic? Did I get the idiot gene too? Do I know enough to teach someone else anything at all? My college major was theatre arts (red wine), so I'm guessing no. I can teach women how to accessorize properly, but I don't think kids need that skill set unless they want to make jewelry out of Legos and convert a Tonka truck into a hat (bragging), and no, Jimmy, I didn't know you already knew how to do that. Eighty-two percent of school children can't locate Wyoming on a map and don't know its total population is 560,000. Would my child be in that eighty-second percentile of kids who can't identify a state nobody can find? How would I explain that at a family reunion (intervention)?

Recently I was at a planetarium with one of my girlfriends and her little boy. She had to stop every five minutes to say things like, "Tommy, this is how the Earth rotates on its axis. Tommy, this is how the moon affects the tides." I was very annoyed at first, but now I'm glad she explained it all to him because now I finally understand it (kind of).

Mothers and fathers tell me the best thing about having kids is reliving their lives through them. Why on Earth would anyone find this an attractive option? Especially school. Who can forget the terror of the rope climb in gym class and the being-scared-to-go-to-the-prom-ness of it all (RIP Carrie)? Homework? I didn't do any the first time around, and now I have to do my child's? It's like an episode of

Punk'd that never ends. And dating? I refuse to relive all those high school relationships (one-night stands).

I was never good with money, unless you count spending it. When I discovered it took $200,000 to raise a child to the age of eighteen, I could hear the door of my vagina permanently slam shut (mostly). I also read that having a baby could lead to heart failure, pulmonary edema, and a ruptured uterus. Even though I didn't know what an edema was, or couldn't locate my uterus on a map of cow udders, that was all the birth control I needed (and the lack of $200,000).

As if all these doubts and fears weren't enough of a warning sign, there was pregnancy. I was the girl who weighed 105 my entire life and still do (lie). So putting on sixty extra pounds was not my secret fantasy. Nausea? I have trouble reading the word "vomit" on a page without gagging and rushing for a toilet bowl.

Women's magazines print serious articles about the beauty of a pregnant woman's enormous belly (oh, please) and her glow. A bride glows, a pregnant woman glows; is there no glow left for the rest of us? And when I read about the pancake-sized nipples that accompany pregnancy, all it does is put me off IHOP for life, which is a pity since that's the only place I really get my glow on.

Who are these women who want to be wide awake during childbirth and, more disturbingly, do it in the bathtub at home? With a woman called a doula telling you how beautiful (repellent) you look and that you only have 1,729 more hours of labor left? I see pictures (mug shots) of these women, and they're pale and have dark circles under their eyes. If I'm going to be spread-eagled in the comfort of my own home and the cameras are rolling, there'd better be makeup involved (and a hairdresser if the venue changes to a local news studio). When I go to the dentist and he pulls out my tooth, I make sure I'm out cold. So why would I be conscious when they pull a seven-pound baby out of me? And my mouth is a lot bigger (I've measured).

If I'd known about the hundreds of times people would ask me about having children, the hundreds of pitiful looks I'd get, the hundreds of *tsk tsks* I'd hear as people walked away, I'd have just answered by tilting my head to the side, sighing deeply, and whispering, "I'm not able to have children" whenever yet another nosy person (Monsignor Caulfield) interrogated me. I consider a colonoscopy less invasive.

People with children are clueless (selfish). They always want to know if they can bring them when they visit me. This is why God invented babysitters. Probably on the eighth day, when he figured out Adam and Eve were missing and presumed they were copulating. I always say "No" because I don't want to live through another afternoon of: "*Put that down. DOWN. So how's your . . . PUT THAT DOWN. What did I just say? Put that down.* Is that a new couch or did you . . . *PICK THAT UP. Pick that up right this instant. Pick that UP.*"

Hey, since that's so much fun, why don't they also bring along those things they simply have to share in yet another text/Tweet/Facebook posting? Like the male dog that favors tall potted plants. And the partly deaf mother-in-law who never wears her hearing aids. And please dip your child in canola oil before you come; I hear that's good for my wood furniture.

There are many alternatives in life. Options, decisions, a path not taken. I don't remember exactly when I decided not to have children, but it was sometime after I briefly considered it at nineteen. Since then, I've never wavered. It's easier to walk away from a potential mistake than to make it in the first place. Every time I see double-wide strollers hogging the slim sidewalks of big cities and the aisles at Target and hear the beseeching pleading of the parents, I know that life choice wasn't for me. And now that I'm at an age where if I started wearing

Gloria Swanson turbans and Ann-Margret caftans, everyone would understand why I eventually took my own life, I ask myself if I have any regrets about not having kids. The answer is no. Although I am worried about who's going to take care of me if I get dementia (although I am worried about who's going to take care of me if I get dementia).

Why I Didn't Have Any Children This Summer

Betsy Salkind

I like children—at least some of them. I don't like them all, but I don't hate them as a group, like some people do, many of whom have children. I'm not even bothered by screaming kids on airplanes; I wish I could do that myself.

I used to think I would end up with a child. Here's how it would happen: I'd open the door one day, and there'd be a baby on the welcome mat. I would close the door, go back inside, and pretend I didn't see it. The next day I would open the door, the baby would still be there, and I'd close the door and pretend I didn't see it. The third day I would open the door, the baby would still be there, and I'd say, "Okay, you can come in." And thus I would adopt a stray child. In this way, I could fulfill part of the adult obligation to help raise the children.

People always say the children are our future, and that always seemed like a false platitude to me until I realized it was quite literal. The children are whom we need to pay for, as they will be paying our Social Security and Medicare, so they really are our future. You'll never hear me complain about paying taxes for schools, despite having no children of my own.

I've always had a fairly dark view of the world and its prospects. Given my sensitivity to the vulnerability of women, children, and animals, I never wanted to be responsible for creating yet another one. For many years, I was not grateful for my own life, and though I am now—it's the only game in town—I'm not attached to life as an idea. Extinction, while sad and scary, doesn't bother me as much as does the suffering of the individuals prior to being wiped out. I oppose global warming because it will cause the suffering of billions, of many species—and I really don't do well in the heat. But I'm not threatened by the idea of humans ceasing to exist. Human life is no more valuable than the life of other species. I cringe when I read about the animals tortured and killed for the sake of humans; and "but they're bred for that" only makes it worse. I feel bad that other people's children and grandchildren may have to live in worse times, but not as bad as I would if I made one myself and had to hear them say, "I didn't ask to be born."

You'd think that people who do have children would take a greater interest in the world of the future, but I'm not seeing that so much. Parents often seem more intent on making sure their kids have advantages over other children than improving the situation for all.

I've also seen plenty of cases where people did not find their own children worthy of attention, or love, or, in some cases, of life itself. I've worked as an activist for child protection legislation and now work with troubled teen girls in a residential facility. I'm a volunteer comedy teacher there, and I love it and I love them, and I'm good at it—for a few hours a week. Some of the girls I work with have children of their own; one fifteen-year-old asked me if I had children. I said, "No." She looked at me as if I had said, "I like to eat babies," and asked, "Why not?" I looked at her aghast. No words came out. She thought I was the fucked-up one.

Sometimes when I say I don't want children, people respond with hostility: "What if everyone took that attitude? The human race would die out!" The human race is more likely to die out from overbreeding as we overstress the world's resources and cook ourselves to death in our waste. But even if everyone stopped breeding—which would be amazing given the regular attacks on contraception and abortion—I would be totally fine with it. It would be a bit of a drag as we all aged at the same time, but it might cut down on elder abuse.

This sense of some mandate to reproduce seems rather outdated to me. When God said be fruitful and multiply, there were only two people. Now there are billions more, and I would say that maxim no longer applies, whether or not you believe in God.

When the McCaugheys had their septuplets in 1997, they kept saying, "God really wanted us to have these seven babies." No, God didn't want you to have *any*. That's why you were infertile. It was Merck who wanted you to have those babies. Children of multiple births tend to be born prematurely, and the children suffer for it with health deficits that often last a lifetime, if they survive at all. (In Germany it's illegal to implant multiple embryos; at least they learned something from their eugenics experience.) In addition, the health care costs are enormous, running into the tens of billions annually in the U.S. alone, a mere fraction being paid for by the parents. God's not paying for it either.

I have no idea what The Learning Channel (TLC) wants us to learn from their multitude of shows about families with multitudes of children, but it seems to be that if you have a few more litters, you can get your own show, and sometimes free houses and diapers. TLC specializes in white American Christian families (*United Bates of America, Kids by the Dozen, 19 Kids and Counting*).[1] They did have one show featuring a large African American family (*One Big Happy Family*), but it wasn't the same: All of the family members were obese, and there were only four of them.

People believe they have a dead fucking right to have kids. You have to have a license to drive a car or to fish, but anyone can have a baby. You should have to pass a test to be a parent. And if you fail, you can take classes, and if you fail again, well . . . let's face it—some people should not be having children. A lot of people should not be having children.

"But who gets to decide?" Me. That could be my service to humanity. I could do a much better job than the self-policing system we currently have. My system would be different from China's, which has produced generations of only children, a huge excess of which are males on account of sexism—which might be less of an issue if homosexuality were embraced. I don't know if this majority of males has anything to do with the large number of stabbings of Chinese elementary school children, but under my plan, that shit would end. On the plus side, China seems to understand that when it comes to reproduction, there's no such thing as a personal decision.

There was a time when people had children to work the fields, but there are very few family farms now, and with child labor laws and all, it's no longer part of our social structure. My brothers and I often thought our parents had us just to work in the yard, but we were an inefficient workforce; having been told to leave the damaged tomatoes in the garden, we stomped on them all. There are many bad reasons to have a child, including "everyone's doing it"; "to have a ready excuse for getting out of any obligation"; "to run for office"; "organs"; and "you need someone with small hands to hook rugs". And if you have kids just so they'll take care of you in your old age, you should keep that in mind while you're raising them.

The only compelling reason I can think of to have one is that you want to contribute to the world by raising some great children. Of course, you don't have to give birth to do this. It's also okay to have a kid if you don't find out you're pregnant until you're in labor (TLC again), or if you're a virgin and find yourself pregnant—then you may want to go ahead and have the baby Jesus.

When I was in fifth grade, I wanted to be a geneticist (and before that I wanted to be president of the United States or a stewardess). I studied Gregor Mendel, and, to demonstrate the laws of genetics, brought a tank of mice I'd accidentally bred to the school science fair. I lost to a kid who'd made a burglar alarm.

Despite my interest in genetics, I never felt a particular attachment to my own genes. Some might consider this low self-esteem; I prefer to think of it as egalitarianism. I oppose breeding, in animals and humans. If you're going to get a pet, take the five-year-old at the shelter, not the purebred from the puppy mill. There are so many homeless and needy animals, why bring more into the world and condemn the others to unnecessary suffering and death? As someone who fantasized I'd been adopted (hasn't everyone who wasn't?), the chromosomal connection to past and future generations is lost on me. Given the mystery of who fucked whom throughout history, I figure we're all related anyway.

Motherhood Once Removed

Judy Morgan

In the 1950s, the American Character Doll Company created Tiny Tears. Advertisements for the doll accurately claimed she could take her bottle, wet her diapers, cry real tears, and give a little girl "the thrill of being a 'make believe' grown-up mother."

Tiny Tears had "rock-a-bye eyes" and could fall asleep. One day, while she napped, I thought about my life. I was nine years old. I could be out riding my bike, or playing with my dog, or reading Nancy Drew mysteries. This pretense, this playing house, left a lot to be desired.

The advertisement's tag line claimed Tiny Tears would be "the gift your little girl will never forget." Truth in advertising. That little doll set me on the right path. Later, it was babysitting that kept me there.

I did well with children who had a two-thousand- to three-thousand-word vocabulary. We'd play games, tell stories, read books. But babies, although cute and likable, were a problem. Their pointing and unintelligible speech—even a parrot knows colors, shapes, and one hundred words in English—left us both frustrated.

I wondered what kind of parents would leave their baby in the care of a fourteen-year-old who had no brothers or sisters. I had never fed a baby, never changed a diaper. Time spent with dolls does not count.

Babysitting, layered with astute observations, caused me to declare, "I may get married someday, although I doubt it. And I will never, never have children." At the time, I was a sophomore at an all-girls Catholic high school in Chicago. When not wearing a school uniform, I dressed in black. I was having a bad year.

Since Grandmother and Mother were present when I made this declaration, introductions are in order. Granny had been married forty-nine years when her husband, my beloved grandpa, died. Together they had eight children. Only five of those children made it to adulthood.

Mom, after twelve years of marriage, had the courage and self-esteem to divorce my father. Imagine a Catholic woman, from a family that did not divorce, filing at a time when divorces were not easily granted.

As I was an infant when their marriage fell apart, I missed all the excitement. But I had the luxury of growing up in a home with two strong women and a grandfather who projected a caring and protective male image. Plenty of aunts, uncles, and cousins completed the picture and made me an only child from a very large family.

Granny's response to my declaration, "Crazy talk," was to be expected. So was Mom's comment, "You might change your mind." Both women, shaped by the times in which they lived, spoke from knowledge and experience.

As part of the next generation, caught in a societal shift, I would have more options than either of them could have dreamed of. My thoughts about marriage and motherhood may have started out as sophomoric, but they developed.

We were advised to pattern our lives after the Virgin Mary. With all due respect, I found very little in her life that was applicable to mine. Unlike the biographies of Clara Barton, Madame Curie, or Eleanor Roosevelt, the life of the Blessed Virgin did not give me a lot to work with.

When I attended a wedding and heard the bride say she would "love, honor, and obey" her husband, it seemed a bit off. Granny and Grandpa were equals. If anything, she made the decisions. Had Mom obeyed Dad, would she have stayed married and tolerated his girlfriend? What nonsense.

Whenever a new cousin was born into the family, it was welcomed with open arms. Literally every female had to hold it. The males were exempt. To pass up that opportunity drew too much attention; the aunts and cousins would get insistent. Better to take a turn.

When the baby was in my arms, it smelled sweet. It was soft and warm. Its tiny features amazed me. I understood and appreciated the miracle of birth, but I did not understand motherhood, nor did I appreciate the overselling of it. To me it was a choice, one of many options. To others it was what women did. We were supposed to breed. It had been decided for us. Society expected it. Religion demanded it.

Most of the women in my family were good mothers and did right by their offspring. Their actions were in keeping with Granny's belief that "you can't give a baby too much love." But there were some women in the family who should have never had children. Being able to procreate does not necessarily mean you should. To quote Margaret Sanger: "Every child a wanted child."

My thoughts on motherhood were not unique. I was not a renegade. I was lucky to be making major life decisions at a time when attitudes were changing. And I was smart enough to know I could not have it all.

Jokes about women going to college only to get an MRS degree had run their course. In 1966, the National Organization of Women was founded. Women had widespread access to reliable contraception. The double standard was in decline. Women were moving into male-dominated professions.

I pursued interests, set and met goals, followed dreams, found employment to fill my wallet, and landed in a profession that fed my soul. And Mom was right. I did change my mind about one thing. My husband and I have been married thirty-five years. But from the start, we were in agreement about not having children. The two of us now act as an extra set of grandparents to all my cousins.

At times my life has seemed scrambled, but there always was a pattern. It became apparent one afternoon while I was eating a slice of plain cheesecake. Concentrating on every bite, breaking down the ingredients, I thought about baking, what it took to bake this luscious dessert. My thoughts expanded to cooking, and cleaning, then sewing, quilting, washing, ironing, and every other activity that has ever been considered women's work.

I could see a parade of women, led by Mom and Granny. They were followed by family and longtime friends: Patricia, Eleanor, Romaine and Edna, Marjorie, Jenny and Josephine. Some were teachers: Sister Agnetta, Sister Rose Dominica, and the always gracious Mrs. Graham. Quite a crowd was gathering.

These women were layered into my life. I had benefitted from their intelligence and independence, their good habits and deeds. They had led by example whether they knew it or not, whether they wanted to or not. I could see myself falling in step with their parade.

Long before I had read Shakespeare's *Hamlet,* Mom would annoy me by saying, "This above all: To thine own self be true." It was her way of calling me on those times when I was not thinking for myself. I'd roll my eyes and, knowing she was right, say the quote along with her in my smart-ass way.

But those words have served me well. Although we may try, we cannot deny who we are. And we are at our best when we are self-defined.

Baby Doubt

Cindy Caponera

When I was approached to write this essay on being child-less, I actually thought it was going to be easy. I'm happily married. I have a satisfying, successful career. I also believed those days of wondering if I missed anything were behind me. All that being true didn't protect me from revisiting my original ambivalence about having children.

As a teen I was obsessed with the fear of giving birth to a down-syndrome or mentally challenged baby—the type of child that would require even more sacrifice than an average child. Given that state of mind, even the idea of a normal baby made me feel I would have to give up everything.

The irony is, I'm great with kids. All kids like me. And all parents like me with their kids. Why I don't have any is still a little bit of a mystery to me, but somehow I knew that having kids was going to get in the way of my big plan. Which was getting out of Canaryville and making a name for myself. It was either that or marrying a guy from Canaryville, living near my parents, and having my own family. Obviously I didn't have much of a plan.

Another barrier to baby was that somewhere deep inside me, I was attached to the idea that you had to hook up with someone first—and for many years I didn't think anyone could love me. So, if you start with a self-hating notion and add on my father's emphatic, nightly resounding dictates of "don't do drugs and don't get pregnant," it's no wonder I was conflicted. My father made me so afraid of getting pregnant as an unmarried woman that oftentimes I would use all birth control methods at once. One time when I told a boyfriend I might be pregnant—after we'd used a condom, the pill, and the sponge—he looked at me like I was insane and basically told me if I was, it came from Jesus.

I was so afraid of sex I didn't even have it until I was twenty. Not to worry; I quickly made up for time lost. That first time, however, I left a Canaryville block party completely hammered, and as I drove to this guy's house, I basically decided I was done being a virgin. After we had sex, I asked if he hated me. He looked at me quizzically. Sometime later I ran into him at the Kentucky Derby. He wasn't as handsome as I remembered.

Very early in my career, I told that story on stage. I thought it was funny because it was so dark and weird. I remember a comedian calling me over afterward. He was a ventriloquist. With a dummy in one hand, he told me how he thought the story of loosing my virginity made the audience uncomfortable. He said it wasn't funny—it was sad. And I should take it out of my act. *Okay,* I thought, *but you have a dummy on your hand.*

Maybe it was the expectation that I *should* have kids as opposed to my actually wanting them that made me feel destined to have them. The quote under my senior yearbook picture read: *I'll stay in and watch your kids while you go out and party.* So obviously I was conflicted even then. And, well into my thirties, when my gynecologist would ask a routine question like, "Do you have children?" I would always turn around to see who he was talking to. I felt like if he actually knew me, he wouldn't ask that question. How could I have a child when I'm living in a five-floor walk-up with a bathroom down the hall? I had so much to accomplish before having children.

And having the skills to do the mom-job was not the issue. I was the fifth of six kids in an Irish/Italian Catholic home. Even though I was on the bottom rung, someone had to take care of my older brothers and little sister when my parents left to party on weekends. My brothers weren't going to do it. So I learned to cook and clean very young. Maybe I felt I'd already put in my time.

I did wind up leaving Canaryville and what I felt were archaic notions and set out on my own. I moved to New York and became a writer, and I'm almost positive I put my shrink's kid through college. But it was all worth it because, it turns out, I did find someone to love me. So then the question of whether or not we were going to have kids became real, not just a conversation you have with girlfriends over wine and cheese. Still, I couldn't get my head around being able to do all of it: having a career and kids, something my mother never had to figure out. Or maybe she did think about it, but it was so far away from what she thought she could ever accomplish that she didn't even try. It would have been impossible for her to step out of her social norms. Hell, I barely got out myself, and I was twenty-six years younger than she was.

Whenever my husband and I are at a dinner party and the subject of children comes up, someone inevitably asks why we don't have any. And without skipping a beat, my husband will reply, "My wife has a bum pussy." After which there is a long silence, then everyone laughs really hard. What they don't know is my husband took that joke from me. But, like all things you sacrifice for your marriage . . . I let him have the joke. And I let him not have kids. Well, that's not entirely true. Initially, I pushed it more, but in the end I think if either one of us had really wanted kids, we could have made that happen. But first I would have to let go of some old ideas. Well . . . one old idea—in the marriage the man makes the money and the woman stays home and takes care of the children.

Somehow I knew my marriage was going to be the opposite. I married a musician, and it wasn't Paul McCartney. I was going to have to earn all the money. That didn't take away from all of the great things he brought to the marriage. I just didn't want to have to go to work while he got to stay home and raise the baby. And I didn't want to have to be the caretaker of everyone else's emotional needs.

And even if we did try, I knew we would have a difficult time making a baby happen, because years before I had been diagnosed with endometriosis—which makes getting pregnant very difficult. Not to mention that we'd married on the later side, so even if we'd done it more and had gotten pregnant, between my dying eggs and his lack of juice, I'm pretty sure I would have given birth to an arm with some hair on it.

We actually considered the adoption route, but that quickly fell away when the first seminar was horror story after horror story of how often the woman you'd invested all kinds of money in would change her mind and keep the baby. I didn't want to allow myself to create and nurture a longing that might never get filled. Plus, you never know what you're going to get. Who wants a Russian kid with no conscience? Had a young Latina girl left a swaddled baby on my doorstep, or perhaps in a bassinette on the 405, I would have picked it up and gladly raised it. We do have that spare room.

I think of my parents and the six kids they had. And I look at my brothers and sisters and all of my friends with kids. And there are a lot of them. I see what kind of work it takes. It's not like when I was little and we played outside after school, came home for dinner, and went out again until the streetlights came on. Now it's all arranged playdates and extreme birthday parties. And when did Halloween get bigger than Christmas?

I remember my mother getting our costumes together. Six kids. Every year at least one of us was Aunt Jemima in a flannel robe and kerchief. She did so much for us. All those lunches she packed and dinners she cooked. All those clothes she bought and washed and folded. All those curtains she cleaned, ironed, and hung every spring and fall in all of our bedrooms. Would I have been willing to do all that work?

Sometimes I think it would be fun to have a kid who's about twenty-one, who I can go out to dinner with, who can help me with my computer and attach my Apple TV Box. I said that to a colleague once, and he replied that what I'm looking for is a friend. It made me laugh. Because he was sort of right. Maybe I wanted a kid I didn't have to be a parent to.

The good news is I can be a friend to all of my nieces and nephews. I can be the person they call when they can't speak to their parents—when they're in trouble. Their Auntie Mame, if you will, as Aunt Joan was in my family. She'd call you a brat then tell you to put your bloody tooth under your pillow so you could get a couple of bucks. She is also the aunt who years later would order me a sweater dryer from QVC and have it sent to my house as a surprise. And currently she's the one who insists on explaining the mysteries of the rosary to me—while I'm trying to jog in the park.

I basically chose my career, waited too long to get pregnant, couldn't have a baby. Didn't want to try that hard. Now it's over, and I like my life. Did I think I was going to like my life without kids before I got here? I don't know. The good news is, I do. So, whatever did or didn't happen, led me to this exact moment.

By not having kids, I've had to have a lot of other experiences to make me grow up. Like my house burning down and having to be the person answering the endless questions while biting my tongue through the insinuations from the insurance people. Wishing instead I could hand the phone to the grown-up—who is now me. Kids give you something to show up for, to fight for. To my detriment, by not having kids I stayed a kid a lot longer than I should have. It reminds me of the old saying "I didn't have a happy childhood, but it sure was a long one."

Some of the things I missed in not having children are mostly intangible. Like experiencing a love so mind-boggling that your heart splits right open. Being afraid for them when they're afraid or taking risks. Cheering for them when they need encouragement. Standing on the shore while they venture out to see how deep they can swim. Letting them know you're there for them when they need you. Choosing to love someone more than yourself.

But the thing I missed the most by not being a mother was more time with my own mother. Had I been a mother, I would have experienced many of the things she experienced. And I wouldn't have wasted as many years not forgiving her sooner for wrongs I perceived she did to me. Things I totally would have done had I had my own children— like being imperfect, or embarrassing them, or making decisions and praying to God they were the right ones. I missed experiencing being a mother with my mother. And now that my mother is gone, and I'm nobody's kid, I wish I could have been hers a little longer. Or I wish we could have been closer sooner. Oh . . . I wish, I wish, I wish . . .

Mommy Boo-Boo

Amy Stiller

"I didn't have an abusive childhood. I had an abusive adulthood." I wrote this recently as a status update on Facebook. "Oh my God! The baby needs to be breast-fed! One minute! I just need to finish this status update!" . . . I could see that happening. Would you want a mother who chose Facebook over your hunger?

But this could be a whole other subject . . .

The truth is, I had a magical childhood filled with Technicolor memories. My brother and me touring with my parents in *The Prisoner of Second Avenue,* imitating their scenes in full costume for the cast, to dazzling laughter and applause! Motels. Hotels. Plastic slides. Club sandwiches and Coca-Cola. John Kenley—the hermaphrodite producer of the Kenley Playhouse in Warren, Ohio, who sang "dirty" songs to us backstage while we attempted to stifle our giggles. Running into Ed Sullivan's arms at six! Meeting the Partridge Family *and* the Brady Bunch! Paul Lynde playing Santa Claus in a bed with my mother as Mrs. Claus in a TV special—hearing him say, "The last time I was in bed with a woman it was my muh-the-e-r." And of course—Uncle Charlie and Aunt Joanie—my parents' glamorous Hollywood actor friends who took us to Disneyland every summer and did magic shows for us at the Magic Castle. He played Marilyn's scared boyfriend on *The Munsters*—it doesn't get any better than that!

I mean, I was so sheltered growing up that by the time I got my first waitress job it was like joining the Peace Corps. The first time I waited on two people who were having a conversation that didn't include me, I was devastated.

How was I supposed to be an adult, get married, and have a child or children when all I wanted to do was to get back to my childhood?

I wanted to be famous because I associated it with that wonderful life. Having a child would be the ultimate defeat.

In my thirties I looked without envy at friends who had kids and were married. They were happy and had careers. They didn't seem to lose their identities. We all grew up in New York City going to private school. We weren't beaten-down female characters in a William Inge play with unrealized dreams longing for fancy coffee in big cities, tethered to three children and faded hunks of husbands named Roy trapped in dead-end lives (even if we'd all done scenes like this in acting classes before the age of twenty-one. Most of my girlfriends have dabbled in acting at some point). But my girlfriends weren't from families like mine. And they didn't end up doing acting professionally like I do. I was a star! My daddy planted this in me from a young age. I was sparkly. I took tap. I had red curly hair, and everyone loved me! What could be better? Even now I feel more like a contemporary with my niece. One day, when I was wearing a very-grown-up fitted blazer with reading glasses with my hair piled high, she looked at me and said, "You know who you remind me of? Miss Hannigan." Then she stopped pensively in her seven-year-oldness and sighed, "No. You remind me of Miss Hannigan *and* Annie."

"Right answer, Ella! Right Answer!"

Does this sound like someone who should be a mother?

Being left behind as "the mother" of someone else? I don't think so! I'm the child, not the mother! Although I am very maternal and have been told that I'm giving. I've also been told that I'm often too giving and do that thing where I see people's potential and don't focus enough on myself . . . so, wouldn't having a child then completely tip the scale toward being the selfless saggy-breasted flabby-bellied gray-haired floppy-faced nonentity giver-person behind the talent? The mother of the Annie Boo-Boo? An unrecognized blob of nothingness and invisibility? The inevitable self-fulfilling destiny predicted by a random gypsy fortune-teller on that broken, desperate PMS day in a Greenwich Village parlor years before?

And yet I'm completely self-involved and have gone to my fair share of "retreats." I would say that the entire eighties were spent being brought to my emotional knees in a desperate attempt to self-soothe through the writing of affirmations; seeking the advice of astrologists, numerologists, tarot readers, and gurus galore; attending spiritual workshops that usually had the word "open" in the title; and signing up for metaphysical newsletters that might have the answer. I remember one that entitled me to a free weekend at an obscure hermitage in upstate New York. My intention was to "reconnect with my authentic self," but I somehow ended up in a sweat lodge with an angry Vietnam vet, two people with self-care issues, a woman with a lot of missing teeth, and a man who was acquitted of murder and had a pardon from Governor

Mario Cuomo framed above the Woodstock poster in his spacious apartment (much larger than mine at the time). He prayed to his higher power to forgive him for the people he had wronged. I prayed for the Meisner technique to unlock my emotional unavailability that fall.

Does this sound like a stable mother to you?

So my point here is that I just never had a desire to have kids. I love kids. I'm a fabulous aunt. I like the idea of being a mother, but as a day-to-day thing . . . it's not for me. I had to lose my innocence to appreciate children's unconditional love. But in my childbearing years, I was still innocent. Still the child. The beauty of Peter Pan is that he got to pretend to play a dad with all the benefits of being a child. It was perfect. Now I'm old enough to play Miss Hannigan. And finally I don't want to be Annie anymore. I would love to play Miss Hannigan to my niece Ella's Annie. It would bring me great joy. I can't sing as well, though. She got that gene from her mom. I'm okay with that. I can let her be the star. I'm ready to be grown-up even if sometimes she's more grown-up than I am.

When she was no more than five years old, while eating a mouthful of spaghetti one evening, out of nowhere, she declared, "Amy." (Sigh.) "If you're an actress, why don't you just *be* an actress. Just do your characters like the ones you do for me." I almost dropped my fork. Immediately I went into my "Hello, Baby Girl" voice (a character that just emerged one day while she and I were hanging out). "Ella, there was this woman who used to say, 'Hello, baby girl', to me whenever I ran into her. And I was well into my thirties. Isn't that crazy! I'm not a baby! She sounded like this: *'Hello, baby girl! Hello, baby girl!'*" Ella makes me do it over and over again. The voice is hilarious, insane, grating, and condescending all at the same time, and she gets it. We laugh hysterically. To be appreciated by a child—that's the thing that makes my adulthood magical.

Buddha and Me

Judy Nielsen

"THE TROUBLE IS YOU THINK YOU HAVE TIME."
—THE BUDDHA

The world was exciting and inviting during those childbearing years . . . so much to explore.

I thought there was plenty of time to have children, so I just thought I would wait, until the right time, the right man, father, partner. That "P" word: *partner*.

In the meantime, there was much to experience: theater, improvisation, being on stage, being in a young, beautiful body. Then, in 1985, as my career was beginning to go up and out, I received a diagnosis of multiple sclerosis. I stopped thinking of childbearing, or thinking at all. I'd always been in my head, always thinking; now my body screamed for attention. Seeing and walking took priority over everything else. A close second was my career as an artist, creating something—other than babies.

After I got the diagnosis, I had a full-time spiritual crisis. Why me? Why now? What's next? What is life? I saw double, but I saw clearly; healing was up to me because there was no God, and Western medicine deemed me incurable. Doctors told me a cure was right around the corner. Now it's 2012, and they're still saying the same thing. It's a mighty big corner.

I followed my intuition and took matters, my matter, into my own hands. I threw myself into healing myself. My ability to live so well with MS for twenty-five years is the result of having had the time and middle-class privilege to heal myself—and of having the *choice* of *not* having children. Luckily, my husband had no interest in having kids either. For that I am forever grateful. No babies.

Instead, I have had time, precious time, to pay attention to *my* eating, *my* sleeping patterns, *my* feelings, *my* dreams. I participated in *my* wellness by committing to the age-old practice of practicing. I practiced t'ai chi. I practiced African drumming. I practiced observing my breath. I practiced not getting pregnant. Taking a sabbatical from Christianity, I wasn't praying. I had become secular, yet my healing couldn't come from modern science. I wanted healing to come from spiritual practices, although I didn't know what constituted spiritual practice.

Seeing myself as a creator—not in the physical sense of birthing another, but in the sense of creating health and wisdom—I became devoted to practice and defining what "spiritual" means.

Healing and gaining strength through stillness, attention, softness, trance, body, worship, and music did not come easily or quickly. To maintain well-being is to maintain those practices that heal body and soul. But practice is practice is practice. I teach those qualities and traditions to receive the benefits long after work hours. I love to teach what I know as wisdom: that which heals me, that which I have committed to practice.

"WE DO NOT NEED MORE KNOWLEDGE BUT MORE WISDOM. WISDOM COMES FROM OUR OWN ATTENTION."
—THE BUDDHA

I always wanted the ability to support myself and any child I would bring into the world, without having to depend on someone else to take half the responsibility, financially or otherwise, if we were to split as a family. After my MS diagnosis, I lost confidence in my ability to juggle both motherhood and a career. I chose my career as it slowly evolved into my healing, then back again into my career, which seemed to be simply living in a body. I made a career of staying in my body, creating a healthful way to live peacefully with MS. But I never felt comfortable providing for myself, much less for another.

In the meantime, I witnessed time and again the agony and ecstasy of childrearing through the lens of others. Watching my friends and family have children, my complaint and pain was that it was boring. I couldn't relate. Of course I would lose friends to their choice to become a householder—creating life, creating a family. I realize bearing children is, for many, the ultimate art: creating a human being. But even if my life was vastly different from the complex relationship of having a family, I wanted to talk to friends about what was important to me. "Hey, I create too, damn it. I create art instead of children."

My passion during prime childbearing years was learning to improvise: on stage, no script, making it up, alone, with others, not trying to be funny, often funny nonetheless.

In 1980, there were very few women learning the longform improvisation called the Harold. It was created by Del Close, one of the originators of The Second City in Chicago. A known misogynist, he was challenging, smart, and talked about tripping, heroin, and, of course, improvising. Improvisation was both thrilling and the ultimate disposable art.

Just for the heck of it, let me consider: What if I had chosen painting as an art form instead of improvisation? Get-togethers would look something like this:

I would bring my paintings with me, everywhere (i.e., when visiting friends or family). In conversation, I would bring up my painting the same number of times my friend referenced her child. In fact I would touch my painting, feed my painting, kiss my painting. I'd work on my painting right there with her, and my friend would work on her creation right there with me present, and we would try to maintain a friendship, or at least an enjoyable visit, adoring our creations together.

However, I wasn't an artist that had something physical as an end product. So sharing what was important to me—my creation, acting, improvising—was challenging. As a result of choosing such vastly different paths of creation, my parental friends and I eventually parted ways. The crowd with which I was creating, other improvisers and performers, made disposable art, and children aren't disposable.

So time flies by. My MS body is in and out of control through the years. I search for my healers and teachers, partners and love. I spend my time trying to heal myself, avoiding the allopathic model like the plague for reasons unknown. I want my healing to come from being devoted to myself, to my deep practice of listening to my body and what it wants, like a mother with her baby. I wanted practices that made me feel alive and well, full and grounded. My t'ai chi chuan and African drumming and Vipassana meditation: They feel as both my mother and my child because of the sheer hours of commitment required; years of devotion. I found movement, music, breath, and Buddha.

Lord knows I love devotion. Not raising a family also allowed me to receive an MA in Religious Studies. Learning about the breadth and depth of patriarchy was a deep piece of inner work and healing. I had time to be intellectual and devotional, contemplative and curious. Many women throughout history have opted to go devotional. Not only for the sake of having time to contemplate, but also to relinquish the joys and sorrows of becoming a householder. My creation became my body, my life in a body.

That's my baby, was my baby, is my baby: devotion to my body and the spiritual longing that is deep within me. Creation has been my response to/need for devotion and spiritual longing. My acts of creation have never taken the form of a human. And I am grateful.

Not Pregnant at the Ob-Gyn

Nancy Van Iderstine

As the youngest of four children born at the tail end of the baby boom, I had lots of plans for my future kids—right up until a few years ago. It never occurred to me that I wouldn't have any. But a couple of lousy choices in men (damn the nineties) and some reproductive system woes later, that's my reality. Or at least it's part of it.

Adoption had never been ruled out until recently, when the demands of my work and involvement in various social, environmental, and animal causes have made that option pretty untenable.

Men and women both joke uneasily about the discomfort of "those" exams at the doctor's office. The nakedness, the cold instruments, being manhandled by someone with whom we *haven't* just had dinner.

Those things don't bother me, but there's a kind of unpleasantness many women experience with the ob-gyn that isn't often discussed. It happens when a woman shows up for checkups time and again without being pregnant.

It is 2006, and I have just navigated around a West Los Angeles traffic snarl to arrive on time for my annual ob-gyn exam. I approach the window at the front desk with a smile and my insurance card. I exchange the card for the sign-in sheet, and the front office worker slams shut the little glass door that separates her from the patients.

The next phase of the yearly ritual is when I hand the pen to the patient in line behind me. If she's pregnant, she will not thank me or smile. In her defense, she may have concerns. She may be frightened. She may not feel well. Which could be my situation as well, of course. Nonetheless, I hand over the pen with a cheery, "Here you go."

I find a chair and smile at the conversation in the waiting room. I find it uplifting to be around pregnant women. They're creating life. They could be carrying a future world leader. Or even a decent bass player. I will *not* be invited into their conversation, however, even as a cheerleader. They seem to intuit my non-pregnancy. Okay, my having a flat tummy may have more to do with that than intuition. But while the ample-bellied ones chat with one another, they completely ignore the woman who's just there for her annual.

After fifty-five minutes of losing myself in Howard Zinn's *A People's History of the United States* (I like light reading in doctors' offices), I am ushered by a dour nurse down a hallway. We pass several dozen photos of reproductive successes. There's one of the doctor proudly displaying a newborn, the jubilant, exhausted mom looking on from behind. There's the three-year-old boy smiling when his baby sister is held up to him. There's the adorable preemie in swaddling. There's the husband in hospital hazmat attire who's just assisted in the delivery.

Past this gauntlet is my designated exam room. I follow the nurse in and carefully set down my purse. Less carefully, she tosses my file on a counter. She takes my blood pressure. I ask what it is, since she won't offer it otherwise. She tells me as she scribbles it on my chart. I say, "Hey, not bad." I want her to agree. I want her to like me, even though I'm not pregnant. I guess I'm hoping for a compliment. I'm in the entertainment business, and yet I have good blood pressure, which I think is an accomplishment. But I get the sense that if the blood pressure weren't good, I'd get scolded. If it is good, who cares? I'm not even pregnant.

Her tone is laconic: "She'll be in in a few minutes. Everything off. Here's the sheet. Here's the gown. It opens in the front."

She leaves. I undress and half cover my nonpregnant body with the pale green waffled paper semi-sheath.

I hear the doctor finish a phone call in another room. "That's great! And the blood work is normal." She's happy. She's loud. Her voice is up an octave. She heads into another exam room. "Hi, Hayley! How are you?" Her pitch is still high. There is laughter. "Well, tell him he'll have to wait a few more months." More laughter, this time louder, from her. From the patient. It's a celebration—someone's pregnant!

Fifteen chilly minutes and a lot of door shutting and phone calling later, I hear the papers shuffle in the plastic file holder on the outside of my exam room.

The door opens. "Hello." The doctor's voice is down an octave. There's no celebration here. No one is pregnant in this room.

Questions about birth control, am I examining my breasts, and any changes in my period are dutifully asked, because they need to be asked. I feel like I've met only the minimum requirements needed to be here—having a period, breasts, and, for a while longer, ovaries.

"Everything looks fine," comes the post-exam summation. "You can get dressed, and I'll see you next year." She's pleasant, polite, and bored.

When the problems with my reproductive system kick in a few months later, they do it with gusto. They begin with a spot of blood heading down the drain during my shower one morning. I'm on the phone with my primary care physician before I even get dressed.

After fitting me into her busy day, she suspects a cervical polyp and wants me to see an ob-gyn. I want a new one. She hands me a list of colleagues she recommends.

"Ha! I'll try Dr. Katz."

"You've heard good things about her, too?"

"No, but I rescue cats, so . . ."

Like voting for three city councilmembers when thirty-eight are running, what do I have to go on other than liking or not liking a name?

After signing in at a front office with no slammable window, I fill out forms and am ushered down another ob-gyn hallway. There is no photo gauntlet. The doors to a few unoccupied exam rooms are open, though, and I can see how they are decorated. One features sea mammals on a wallpaper border, one has goofy black-and-white cow patches painted on one of the walls, and the one I wind up in is crazy with cowboy hats and horseshoes. Dr. Katz has a thriving ob-gyn practice. She's also an animal lover.

Ten minutes later, the boisterous doctor bounds into the room with my chart. During the exam, I relate that my last period was exhausting and unusually crampy. As a precaution, Dr. Katz phones a radiologist.

Nothing much crosses my mind during the next three days. It's just one of those weird things.

The radiologist is a sweet guy who apologizes for the cold jelly on my belly and the invasive nature of the exam. But his compassion is more notably revealed by the look on his face when he sees the image of my abdomen on his screen. He opens his mouth to ask something when I leap in with, "Did you ever see *Alien*? So scary!" Like a lot of women, I want to put people at ease when I realize they're uncomfortable, even if their discomfort has to do with my own suffering.

"Are you in pain?" he then asks, rather quietly.

"Not normally, but things have been a little uncomfortable lately."

When the diagnosis is complete, the findings are, in alphabetical order: endometriomal cysts (on both ovaries), endometriosis (freestyle), fibroids, and an enlarged and tipped uterus, for added drama. Maybe another polyp or two. The cysts are the big worry. We will wait five weeks and hope the cysts shrink on their own.

Given what was happening, who knows why I hadn't experienced many symptoms. Or had I, but had I also bought into thinking that, since I wasn't pregnant, I had no right to give importance to my pain and fatigue?

Work is very busy, and I don't find the time to explore whether alternative medicine might help downsize the cysts. Five weeks later, another ultrasound reveals one of the cysts has grown.

Back in her office, Dr. Katz whips out a laminated anatomy graphic that we use to discuss what's likely to be removed. Since there is a cancer scare, it's out with the uterus, fallopian tubes, ovaries and their new pals, the cysts, along the cervix, probably.

My mother offers to fly out for a week. She is a tremendous help, and even makes me laugh as I'm being wheeled atop the gurney toward the OR, as she chimes in with: "Oh, I forgot the camera!"

Post-op, I learn my uppity cervix refused the knife and so remains intact, its own little gateway to nowhere. The recovery room technician explains I can request a "blood patch," since the epidural didn't go well and I have a horrific spinal headache. I choose not to give the anesthesiologist another stab at things, although my mother later notes that the technician is a hottie.

"But think about what he's seen of me, Mom."

It's been nearly seven years since the hysterectomy. Though it's tragic the operation punctuated my not having children, I have managed to find peace of mind in not being a mother. My interactions with young relatives and friends' kids has helped. And for every child I haven't had, I have fostered and placed in permanent homes several homeless animals, who continue to find their way into my heart—and my apartment!

Now, when I go in for my annual exam, I am asked how I'm doing. Has my lack of reproductive organs elevated me on the compassion scale? Is it because those organs finally *did something?* Were they and I previously viewed as being lazy? More likely, things have just improved because I found a doctor who respects the nonpregnant. While Dr. Katz also has many photos of her deliveries, she keeps them in her office, not on a gauntlet wall. Some of the photos are hilarious—she's wearing a cowboy hat in one, she's hoisting up a mighty placenta in another. She also has a photo from her wedding day in which she and her husband are surrounded by their many rescued pets.

My doctor has also never had children, and she has had a hysterectomy. We have commiserated about the shocks of sudden menopause and laughed about how handy hot flashes can be in the winter. She asks what projects I'm working on, and congratulates me on my still-fabulous blood pressure. Not to mention she kept my belly ring intact.

All this—even though I'm never pregnant.

Alice in Brazil

Nancy Shayne

I have always had an attraction toward inanimate objects. I can still feel my four-year-old hands reaching down into the box of Cracker Jack to find the secret prize. This was far more exciting than eating the candy-coated popcorn. I knew that within seconds, I would be holding something wonderful that was mine and mine alone. And when I touched the magical prize, it would prove to develop its own personality by the sheer fact that the prize from the Cracker Jack box was in my hand. We would go through life together and mature. I had a reason to live.

My particular reason to live was a one-and-a-third-inch plastic dog charm covered in a cellophane wrapper. When I took the wrapper off him, I knew he was blessed to have me as his one and only dog mother.

He was red, so I named him Reddy. Later that day, I hit the jackpot and pulled out yet another prize from another Cracker Jack box that turned out to be a dog as well. He was green. I named him Greeny. Greeny was big, and Reddy was small.

For the entire year that I remained a four-year-old girl, I never let Reddy and Greeny out of my hand. They went everywhere with me. We slept together, bathed together, and ate Kraft Macaroni and Cheese together. They attended prekindergarten and synagogue on Saturdays, and they enjoyed summer camp. I was identified as that little hopeful but scared kid who had to hold toys in her hand in order to feel safe. But to me, I was just being a good plastic dog mother, because plastic dog babies must be taken care of.

On a freezing winter day shortly after I turned five years old, my best friend's mother wanted to take pictures of her daughter and me having fun in the snow wearing our ill-fitting snow suits with oversized mittens. We smiled, but we were not having fun. We were freezing five-year-olds on a tiny lawn with one tree per house in a postwar suburb trying to please adults who want to believe that all kids enjoy the thrill of making snowballs and smashing them into each other's faces. As I smiled for the camera trying to please the adult world somehow Reddy and Greeny slipped out of my hand and fell in the snow.

I never saw them again.

I tried to believe that when spring came and the snow melted, they would show up on the grass. They would be there because, although battered by winter, they were strong plastic dogs that needed to wait for their mother to wash them and hold them in her hand once again and protect them from the harsh elements of life. As the seasons passed and I became an old girl of nine, I understood that with each melting snow, my wish would not be satisfied. Instead I would become the baby boomer secretly believing that Reddy and Greeny managed to find their way to the eBay collectibles site under the category of Cracker Jack Plastic Prizes from the 1950s—and my plastic-obsession pain would be lifted when I saw how safe they were on cyberspace waiting for me to pick them up.

I cannot remember the distance between the loss of Reddy and Greeny and my next obsession, but she was found in a display in the five-and-dime store that said DISNEYKINS—MINIATURES! COLLECT THEM ALL! As a little girl, I was in love with the Disney cartoon *Alice in Wonderland* and believed that if you were as pretty and clever as Alice, flowers would actually sing to you if only you posed the right questions. The Alice in the display was ten cents, and the reason why she was so expensive was because she was made out of hard plastic and was hand painted by great artists in Hong Kong. I know this because there was a sticker at the bottom of the base of the figurine that said HAND PAINTED IN HONG KONG. Her eyes were dot eyes, and they were black. Her lips were a red dot, and she wore a blue-and-white dress and had little white socks and shoes. She leaned forward a bit, which I always felt was a mistake in the design department, but the mistake made her more vulnerable and beautiful. Alice had survived vitriolic queens, scabrous rabbits, and Mad Hatters. She had been down the rabbit hole and back. And now she was mine, and we would go on further journeys, but this time they would be far more pleasant than the ones she had known.

Alice never left my side or my hand for two years. She sat on my desk in elementary school in third grade and read the same books I read. I made her miniature versions of textbooks that said BASIC MATH, SCIENCE, and THE HISTORY OF WESTERN EUROPE. She was so extraordinary. In fact, she was so extraordinary that when we were asked to take one month and go to the library to research any country in the world to write a school report, we decided that it might be exciting to research the dark continent of Africa where everyone has drums and wears colorful clothes. But then we came up with a better idea. We picked the country of Haiti because it lived in the ocean in an unknown area. And the name Haiti was cute. Alice helped me read books about the products that Haiti exported and imported and helped me tell the class that Haiti was ruled by an evil dictator.

When I went to California to visit my aunt on a train that summer, I knew that Alice could develop motion sickness, so I begrudgingly agreed to give her to my best friend, Fern, who said she would watch over Alice until I returned one month later. She said she would be the keeper of all of Alice's books and make sure that Alice was well taken care of.

When I returned from California, the land of oranges and sun, I ran to Fern's house on a rainy day and knocked on the door knowing she would open it with Alice in her hand and tell me of her adventures before I talked of my own.

"Alice is in Brazil," Fern said.

"What?"

She's visiting the rain forest. She's on vacation."

"You don't have Alice?" I asked.

"She's in Brazil," she repeated with resolve.

Alice had fallen down a drain while Fern was taking a bath. She just didn't know how to tell me until we were in our late twenties, when she believed I was strong enough to finally accept that my beloved one-and-three-quarter-inch plastic object with a beautiful mouth and delicate hands and a fine personality was just a piece of plastic. An assorted composite of resins produced in Korea or Hong Kong.

We were now adults. We were adults that should laugh about our former attachments. Adults who most likely according to the popular world should stop speaking of all things magical and unreal and concentrate on finding a good man and having good babies who will grow up to be good kids with a proper amount of fantasy and then, slowly, just like their mothers—outgrow it.

And I suppose I outgrew it. Not in the traditional sense that involved raising a child that burped, cried, needed private school as opposed to public school, or had opinions as to which relatives they preferred. But I did develop a strong need to love. So I made the great leap and took home a puppy. I raised Willie Bean from eight weeks of age until his untimely death from cancer at seven years old. Since I had become an expert as a child mourning the loss of inanimate objects, now I became an expert in my inability to handle the death of my dog and only let him go long, long after he was gone. I can still hear his bark, the sound of his paws, his breath, his snorts, and, most of all, the sound he made when he savagely grabbed treats from me and then looked through me as though he knew I had just been devoured with his love.

Love. Of course that is all there is.

With no judgments.

When a friend of mine adopted a baby at a very late age, she said, "I finally realized that motherhood was all there was worth living for. And I'm now going to cradle her in my arms."

And I thought to myself, *Good for you. Cradling your baby in your arms is nice.*

As for me, I'm about to cradle my imagination in my hands. With a firm grip.

And if I'm patient enough—Alice in Wonderland just might return after decades from her travels in Brazil and have a cup of tea with me. Reddy and Greeny might miraculously show up after being lost in the snow for so long. And, somewhere in the vast universe, Willie Bean is waiting for me to join him.

Why I Am "Barren"

Vanda Mikoloski

"Hi Vanda, it's your mom!" A chipper voice wakes me from my late morning doze. "Ya still barren?" My mom loves this joke from my stand-up act, where I make fun of how awful that word sounds. "Barren," I say, "like my womb's a dustbowl . . . dirt and tumbleweeds blowing about. I open my legs and you hear the theme from *The Good, the Bad and the Ugly:* Woo-ooo woo-ooo, ooo ooo ooooo ooo . . .

"Yes, Mom," I say. "Still barren. My womb is fallow. In fact, I've been thrown on the scrapheap of old spinsters. I'm talking to you on my cell phone from the Los Angeles Spinster Heap. I'm supine on a pile of half-alive, useless crones, of no value anymore to the tribe. We can't even chew leather to soften it, Mom. We can only gum the leather."

"Oh, Vanda Mary!"

My mom, Mrs. Dorothy "Dotty" Elaine Robinson Mikoloski, became a mother during the 1950s. Within three years, she gave birth to my brothers Bryan and Pavel, and then to me on June 26, 1959. My sister, Andria, came along four years later.

"Your mom had Fifties Damage!" a psychotherapist friend said recently. "The main symptom of F.D.," she joked, "is ennui . . . the idea that this is all there is, and all there is isn't all that great." I do remember my mom doing laundry for six in our dank basement, deeply depressed. She'd match endless pairs of socks while the radio played Peggy Lee's existentialist hit, "Is That All There Is?" Then she'd bang the pots and pans passive-aggressively as she made dinner, trapped in the life that was supposed to have brought joy. At ten, I decided I was never going to be that miserable.

"All I ever wanted was a nice family," my mom said recently as I visited her in Baltimore, where she lives by herself, a vital seventy-eight-year-old. She had *not* foreseen a domineering, alcoholic, and largely absent husband, hyperactive and untreated rebellious children, intrusive Polish in-laws, WASP-y New England neighbors who hated us newly wealthy Polacks, or the painful losses to come.

A few short years later, in what was to become one of the two central dramas of my mom's and my life, my big brother, Bryan, fifteen, drowned in the town reservoir while "huffing" aerosol spray and swimming with a group of friends.

It was around that time I took LSD and sat on a hill looking over the high school football field. I had a good trip. I saw that my parents had it all wrong. They believed the dictate "Don't be you because you suck" that hides in the wallpaper of too many all-American homes, and all of our systems, if you think about it: education, religion, medicine, law, family, sports, politics, advertising, you name it. Being authentic was a hindrance. And I saw heaven that day. I saw Truth. For the briefest instant, I became *one* with a tree. I saw that I was a perfect, whole, and complete child of the Universe. I so wanted to run home and tell my parents they were misinformed. I actually felt compassion for them. Thank God they weren't home that day, as the message of Universal Love from their tripping teenager probably wouldn't have been happy news.

Although devoted to clean living now, I will say that drugs saved my young life, giving me a perspective I never forgot that ultimately pulled me away from the barstool and the coke. There was something awe-inspiring about life and about me. Perhaps we ought to rethink the "Just say no" thing in some cases: You know, "Just say no to bad drugs," something like that.

Three years after my brother's death, my dad died in an alcohol-related car accident at age forty-eight. My dad, whom I loved/hated. My dad, who showed me how to fertilize plants organically and how to ride a horse ("Show 'em who's boss, Van!") My drunken dad, who taught my brother "boxing" ("Fight like a man, Bry!") until he bled.

There's a demolishing of something vague inside, a sparse landscape that burns, when you don't process the sadness and anger and confusion of death. I didn't really know what it was, and I didn't know how to get to it. There was a white-hot flame inside me that I didn't want to touch. The best I could do was try to close my heart quietly like a door and slip away.

As I moved into my twenties and thirties, the idea of having children just never really entered into the picture. True to my decision at age ten, I spent most of those years not being miserable. I was a "party girl" . . . and then later a "party woman"—which never looks good on anybody. I felt like Charles Bukowski, but pretty. I used alcohol, illegal substances, and other wounded people to distract me from my feelings.

This was before we knew cocaine and sex could kill you. And a little after. Well, a lot after. Birth control was whatever I had on hand, and if that didn't work, abortion. I was always too selfish, drunk, irresponsible, and fuck-you independent to even consider having a child.

I found it easier to take off my clothes than to take off my emotional armor. It was easier to open my legs than to risk opening my heart, to bare my body than bare my soul. I couldn't even distinguish the armor, really. It just seemed that a lot of undesirable guys were showing up. Fourteen in a row one year, back-to-back, no sherbet in between to cleanse the palette. It is fashionable for female comics to complain about how bad men are and dating is. In reality, I hung out with the most interesting, fun, smart, funny, and neurotic men on the planet. I yearned to be a part of some great guy's life, but I somehow ended up over and over in relationships that seemed like jokes. It felt sort of normal. So did the sex, drugs, comedy, alcohol, spirituality, more alcohol, and even the jokes.

The last time I had the chance of escaping the prognosis "barren," I was forty and drunk at some Bacchanalian wine fest held at "channeler" JZ Knight's ranch in Yelm, Washington. I stayed on a bender for several weeks after the event and, before long, morning nausea alerted me to the fact I was pregnant. Slumped against the wall of my living room, I sat on the wine-stained carpet and I cried. The handsome, Chinese-Dutch photographer with whom I'd had sex could have made an okay dad, I guess. Really, though, he was broke and I was broke and I was a mess. I also didn't think a man would ever love me enough to want me to have his child. I wasn't lovable; I was leaveable.

Finally, alcohol almost killed me. My "bottom" had to do with a year of small humiliations and two DUIs in a row. Finally, exhausted, I went to a poorly funded, state-run rehab. But even within my humility, I was still a know-it-all. I was called "movie star" by the staff—not a compliment—because I put on makeup and did my hair every day to impress the men in "group." I endeavored to coach the counselors on what they should teach about nutrition, the relationship of alcoholism to blood sugar imbalances, and of course organic. I knew a lot about organic. It is so what alcoholics laugh about when they are on the other side of using: that they would be so close to death, giving a lecture to healthy people on the benefits of eating healthy. Somehow, however, enough humility and surrender actually did sneak in. Why was I drinking myself to death? Was I an irresponsible, self-destructive asshole? Am I anesthetizing some old wound? I began to reach out to friends and look underneath the rock of my self-numbing.

I became willing to be uncomfortable. To look at some of the "winning" strategies that had helped me survive my childhood but that ultimately would take me OUT if I continued with them. These last ten years of sobriety have been a process of reclaiming my life and learning to feel the discomfort of my feelings. I began to look at what I really wanted my life to be for. What kind of life could I design that is worthy of this gift of life? Author Eckhart Tolle writes of a hyphen between the years of one's birth and death on one's gravestone. I want a kick-ass hyphen. I want to be a life-giver to the world. I have begun "checking in," as they said in the sixties, rather than checking out.

Now that I am sober and fifty-three and just humming in my career and my relationships, I entertain discomfort when I am awake enough to do so. I sit with my little sadnesses and enjoy them, watch them wash through me, becoming nothing but sensation, vitally alive, raw life itself. Even this morning, in my yoga practice, tears came on and off for ninety straight minutes. I was dipping in and out of what seemed like a fathomless pool of sadness and loss, trying to cry discreetly. It's still there. It's like an old sports injury. It kicks in when I do something to agitate it. The difference now is I observe my urge to distract or anesthetize. And it's just pain, not suffering.

My mom and I talk about Bryan and dad, and the tears come. Life "lifed" us. We are a family left reeling by life. We've recovered to the degrees we have. Some of us have accepted death, and some of us still harbor deep sorrow and guilt. That great "shouldn't have happened" . . . that great *"Why?"* my mother wants to scream at God, and at the unbearably blasé Universe that didn't even miss one fucking beat when her child died. Rivers still roll. Bees buzz. The pain hurts so bad at first, but I open to the indifference now. My favorite spiritual teacher, Byron Katie, says, "My God is reality because it rules, but only 100 percent of the time." My path is now a path of living in harmony with what is, no matter what it is.

I forgive myself. Again and again if need be. And others. We all beat up on ourselves; hell, a lot of us beat up on our children. I do not listen to the voices that tell me I am inferior nearly as much as I used to.

I let my mom off the hook. My mom flew in recently from Baltimore to Sedona to see a movie I was making with a group of great guys. She watched me, pregnant with ideas, producing a movie. Although we are polar opposites still, we love each other deeply and talk on the phone weekly. She wishes she could have been a better mom and that I could have had a more "normal" life. What is a normal life? My mom did what she did. I did what I did. She raised four humans. The idea of doing that does appeal to me, but it looks like I'm going to be using my life-giving skills elsewhere. I'm a natural teacher, healer, nurturer; and I'm hysterical onstage. I'll give life, all right. I'll create culture.

Bearing It

Wendy Liebman

When my husband and I are making out, and he whispers, "Oh, baby—oh baby," I shout *"No baby—no baby!"*

Don't get me wrong. I *love* babies. I think babies are the cutest people in the world. Even the ones that look like Troll dolls. I love how soft they are, their pudgy little legs, how perfect their hair is, and their straightforward agenda: eat, suck, pee, poo, cry, sleep. Repeat. Everything they do is monosyllabic! I love that! And I love when babies smile. And after they're all clean and powdery, I love the way they smell. My heart bursts open for every baby!

And emotionally and financially, I'll be ready to have one of my very own in about five years. But the joke's on me—I've *already* gone through "the change." (I don't mean getting into yoga and buying a black Thunderbird convertible.) The carton is empty; my eggs are powdered. It's too late, baby. The hands on my biological clock just gave me the finger. *"No baby"* is no longer shrieked, but said with resolve, with my head down in a tiny, solemn voice.

I already have two teenage stepsons who refer to me as "the lady in the kitchen who doesn't know how to cook." I moved in when they were four and eight. Now they are more than six feet tall, smart and sweet and über-talented. They make me proud, they make me laugh, push my buttons, teach me everything I need to know (except how to cook), and basically rock my world.

But I didn't bear them. I raised them, and they are two of the people I love the most. But they're not my flesh and blood. Milk. Eggs. They got my nurture, not my nature. Sure, I didn't get stretch marks. Sure, I got two amazing stepkids. But I didn't get a baby to call my own.

Sigh.

The thought of being a mother has always been inconceivable (pun intended) to me. I flirted with the idea from time to time in my thirties and forties, but I quickly realized I really only wanted a child so I could see 1) what it would look like, and 2) how funny it would be. Also so I could shop for miniature shoes. (i.e. self centered reasons.)

Like women who give up their careers to have children, I basically gave up my children for my career, and by "gave up my children for my career," I mean "didn't really ever entertain the thought of having them." I was too busy entertaining—telling jokes—sometimes about just this topic, laughing with others instead of crying alone.[1]

There *was* a time right after college, before I started doing stand-up, when all I could think about, and I mean *all*, was having a child. I even read through the catalogues, picked out strollers, mobiles, the stencil pattern, the college. I was *all* "baby this!" and "baby that!" I was cer-ti-fi-ably *obsessed*. And I drove everyone around me crazy! Not to mention myself! I really really really really really really really really really really really really really wanted a child. I was twenty-three. It lasted six minutes.

But then I realized I would have to be pregnant. (After having to *get* pregnant.) And except that it would allow me to eat for two, I *never* wanted to be pregnant. (Did the Octomom eat for nine?) My sister, she's a shrink (and she's four foot eleven), loves being pregnant. She swears by it. I would just be swearing. I am daunted at the thought of carrying another person inside of me like a Russian Nesting Doll for nine months. I don't even like feeling full after dinner.

Of course I could have adopted, but if I was going to take care of another person, I wanted it to be *mine*. Because I'd heard that absolutely nothing compares to the experience of having a child. (Not the actual birthing process—I've heard that that's like "shitting a tractor."[2]) I've heard that creating another human being makes you believe in miracles. Nothing compares to it. I've also heard that nothing compares to getting a spike through your head, though I question the source.[3]

On the flip side of me being too egotistical to be a mother, I know I would also be too anxious and immature for the role. A mother does *everything*. Period. Feed, clothe, and shelter. Help them sleep. Guide them to make good choices, share stories. Pass down information. Support them financially until they're thirty-five.

Not to mention the responsibility of naming someone! Giving the world *one word* to call another human being until they were old enough to change it through the legal system was way too much pressure for me.

In my "*to baby* or *not to baby*" debate, *no* outweighed the *baby* (which is somewhere around six pounds, seven ounces) because of all of the reasons above, *plus* I'm too sensitive. I wouldn't be able to take my kids' vitriol. I dreaded the day when one of them screamed at me, "You don't understand anything, Grandma!" I wouldn't be able to take their criticism. Their intimacy. Their dependence. Their shit. That grandma thing. I was working on all of that in therapy, but I was completely out of sync. In this case, my timing sucked. And now I have post-nopartum depression.

I try to focus on the positive: I never had morning sickness (except once when hungover). I never had to lose the baby weight *or* my virginity. And I'm grateful beyond words for my stepsons. *They* make me believe in the divine. They might not have my DNA but they have my *haha*! And they totally have my heart! Now if they just knew my name . . .

I still periodically fantasize about my own baby, though. In my "infant-asy," all of my self-centeredness, puerility, and insecurity are transformed into care and concern. I worry about my offspring, 24/7. I try to control every aspect of my baby's world forever to ensure they are healthy and happy, safe and secure. I would be insanely overprotective, to the point that, basically, I would never let my child outside . . . of my body.

And essentially, that's what I've done.

Who Shall Bear Witness?

Jeanette Schwaba Vigne

O ne of my sisters never fails to remind me, albeit unconsciously, that *everything* she has learned that is *really important* is because of her kids. She says her children are her teachers, and are so wise! She was saying this when they were four, by the way. I don't know how many times I have heard her refer to them as "elegant souls." I guess my soul must be slovenly with poor posture and big hair, wearing eighties clothing from the fine designers at Walmart or Goodwill, whereas their souls are all fine-featured little ballerina Audrey Hepburns in Polo.

Don't get me wrong. I think children are adorable, but you know they can grow up to be serial killers and terrorists. Some children are dangerous from the beginning, definitely some who lived in my neighborhood. Marty Maloney stole pets and bicycles that were never again the same, when or if returned. Then there were the O'Herny boys, all in law enforcement now, which is a frightening thought considering their history of aggression and violence and their childhood penchant for torture.

Among my numerous siblings, there's this unspoken idea that because I don't have kids, I'm a tad selfish, immature, irresponsible. Well, I admit I am selfish and irresponsible . . . a tad. But at least I'm a tad responsible and selfless enough to know that perhaps it's better for me *not* to bring another selfish and irresponsible minimee into the world.

But am I a failure as a woman because this child, this raison d'être, is missing from my life? What *is* missing in me is the biological urge to procreate—the overwhelming desire to have a baby has never really existed for me.

All right, maybe when I was eleven years old and saw Franco Zeffirelli's *Romeo and Juliet* and wished I could be married to Romeo, played by Leonard Whiting, but even then there was no chance since Romeo dies (oops—spoiler!). But this only fueled my never-ending love for Romeo and the wish that at least we could have had a child together. But it would have been totally impossible since at that time, I wasn't even menstruating yet. However, I really do love Shakespeare because of this, and I suppose that is edifying. Ah, those child star-crossed lovers who can teach the world a thing or two. Children are so *wise,* aren't they? (Please excuse this interruption by my sister; back to the regularly scheduled program.)

I admit I'm curious about the missing urge to procreate. Mildly curious. I like fine things; I like beautiful looking shoes that will cripple your spine later on. I've put many a toxic chemical on my hair, and I've tortured my body in the pursuit of beauty, to be "attractive." But for what end if it was not to attract or lure a man and make him my lifelong love slave by having children with him? I do enjoy the romance and the sex given the right supplier, but by many accounts, the baby dear will usually blast that stuff away anyway.

And I've seen the photos of couples—before kids and after kids. I observe this evident shift where the woman seems to be the general and the father some kind of underling soldier. Or, there's the highly domesticated Mr. Moms carrying babies in sling-type chest packs, drinking coffee outside of Starbucks, probably sexting with the ex–high school flame they reconnected with on Facebook. Usually, the unsuspecting wife is a hardworking business woman and the father is an unemployed doofus or artist of some kind. One and the same, says one friend.

In a couple years he will have to endure the toddler stage and afternoons in the park with the golden retriever watching his adorable children play, and sexy young moms being overly helpful—which he takes advantage of—and finding him charming and sweet despite the unspoken societal opinion that he's been emasculated. Later, his hardworking wife will return home after a grueling day at the office and clean the house and cook dinner since he's had the kids all day and now he needs a break. Of course, I exaggerate and grossly generalize, sort of.

Some of my child-bearing friends appear to be having a sloppy good time, and others are just waiting for the day the little dears will graduate college, which there is no way they can afford—or maybe they can get a good job in the future, such as mowing lawns and blowing leaves, since all of the white-collar jobs will be in India and China.

Do global warming and the economy ever come into their minds when they're ovulating and saying, "Now, honey! We've got an hour!" By the way, I was married for almost seventeen years, and I could never bring myself to call him "honey," which still seems so suburban and unoriginal to me. Did you ever notice it is often spoken with underlying menace by one or the other parents? But that is another topic . . . sort of.

Culturally it is implied that there is something wrong with women who don't have kids—the old biblical idea that we and therefore our lives are "barren." Mothers talking about their children is an experience so absolutely barren of interest for me that I am overcome with ennui and an utter depletion of energy . . . that is, unless the children being discussed are drug addicts who've just stolen the nasty neighbor's hideous Grecian statue from the front lawn to supply their habit—then I perk right up.

Even when mothers aren't sharing stories of their devil spawn, they still find sneaky ways to brag about their progeny, slyly taking credit for creating the most spiritually evolved enlightened human being to grace the Earth. Lisa Garr from the radio program *The Aware Show* should take note; I have to turn the dial when she goes on about her little angel.

Okay, I admit to being a child once, and a very good child. But only because I was terrified most of the time. I tried being bad, but I was so bad at being bad that nobody even noticed. When I was twelve, I had to call my mother at four in the morning to tell her I was tripping on Orange Sunshine, and then she wanted me to rat on my dangerous connection and dealer, who was the coolest and most highly delinquent kid from the wealthiest community in the country, Kennelworth.

His name was Tommy O'Rourke, and he was thirteen. First time I've ever admitted his name! Word was he got caught several times throughout his teen and college years without ever having to serve time. Word *is* that he's a highly successful CEO now, I believe at Monsanto. He was a very "bad" boy. However, please don't draw the conclusion that horrid monstrous children grow up to be successful adults. Well, you can if you want.

Of course, it's not unusual for "good" children to grow up to be repressed highly neurotic depressed unfulfilled adults. What good did it do me being "good"? I'm still being good. Here I am, a middle-aged woman, now caring for my mother out of obligation (and yes, love), but also because I am still being "good." (And because others can't do it because they find the Midwest "depressing.")

Then my little sister was burdened with the caretaking role for several years, just like in the Middle Ages where the youngest sacrifices her life to take care of the parents, but she finally escaped. She ran off with an artist, changed her name and identity, and was last seen in an ashram on the highest mountains in Tibet. She is now known as Luminia Placentia, and her children are in spirit only, as they are guides from the Xeniaphonia galaxy, which is terribly far away, unless you meditate enough.

But with all the children my mother has had, in her time of need, as she is reverting back to the second childhood of old age, I am wondering, where is everybody? Where are all her other children? What happened to the other five brothers and sisters, besides me and Luminia, to share this caretaking? Gosh, I can't help thinking: If I am fortunate enough to live long enough to need a wheelchair and a translator for my encroaching dementia, who will be there to help me?

I guess I'm grateful for not having to lay a sense of guilt and obligation on my unborn progeny, who might resent me for it, and be really pissed off at what my generation has done to the planet. And really, why would I want to bring an innocent into this hostile and overpopulated environment? Because of my "urges"? Isn't *that* selfish?

Scientists say our "urges" are about keeping the species going. But that just seems . . . oh, so Neanderthal. I wonder if maybe the pinnacle of evolution is ultimately mass extinction. After all, mass extinction is not dramatic without the masses. We certainly do seem to be generating enough people for the sizable armies necessary for the ever-increasing wars, right?

In my present "barren" state, I look at the pleasantness of the ever-increasingly heated world around me, with twenty species dying every day, and the delightfully optimistic predictions that the "new wars will be fought over water, not oil!" I imagine singing this peaceful lullaby to my little newborn (music box music in background—you know, that Tinker Bell type):

Welcome to Earth my little darling—once the land of abundance and fertility, now a barren and hostile landscape thanks to our infinitely multiplying species voraciously using up all natural resources, all to maintain our lifestyle of consumption.

Today, my wise little minimee, we will stroll in your high-tech BMW *baby carriage through mini-China in Walmart! Next we'll hit Target, and Costco, and Cost Plus World Market, and babyGap! Then we'll take a break at Starbucks, and I'll buy you a triple fair-trade hot cocoa with genetically modified soy milk to ensure you reach puberty by age four, and enough sugar to make sure that your* ADHD *is intense enough to feed you a drug (Mierdia?) that I saw the other night on* Housewives of the Apocalypse. *I myself will have my triple nonfat latte (when is Starbucks ever going to get organic milk?!), and I'll get buzzed enough to continue shopping and perfecting the pursuit of stuff, because it shows I care, and besides . . . I can't deprive my little darling of stuff. We're saving the economy by shopping and all, which is far more important than life, including you my little darling. Kootchie kootchie coo.*

And when I get home I'll fix myself a stiff Ketel One martini with fresh lime and fresh ginger, to swallow down Prozac and Xanax to handle the very full emptiness of my stuffed life.

But you know, now many parents think their children are here to change the world and rescue us all. They created these little geniuses to "invent inventions," says a jewelry-laden Lexus-SUV-hybrid-driving soccer mom, "that will restore the balance of the planet" and apparently make it more hospitable. These little Einsteins, given the appropriate dosages of Mozart, will restore balance and harmony to Mama Earth, and that is why they were born . . . they are called the Indigo Children.

Apparently, these new special children are here to carry us to the next step of evolution yada yada yada . . . which makes me think of my sister who is in Italy with her children at this time, on their sixth vacation of the year. "Because they absorb information like a sponge. Because they are brilliant! Al and I are so proud of them!" she says to me, the poor unfortunate childless sister. Implication is, the parents must be pretty damn special for creating these pretty damn special children.

I want to tell her, but never will, that no matter what she thinks or believes, her children may not be highly evolved, enlightened, special, or the Indigo Children, a child cult that wants to tear apart the current fabric of society, which is actually fine with me.

I want to say, "Your children are fortunate because you have a lot of money and time, because you married well and have access to the best and can take your children to France to learn French, Spain to learn Spanish, England to learn English . . . and yes, even Sicilia, ancestral home of their father whose infinite wealth is a mystery, to learn Sicilian . . ." But I don't say it. I bite my lip and hope it swells to a bee-sting pout.

Even though I was once happily married but now am not, I am not barren. I chose to be alone, and I will live in places where the Earth cracks open, or the waters rise, threatening to swallow the corrugated shacks and homemade tents where we plain "folk" share our bootleg water, places where even the private armies of the elite dare not enter.

And should I live long enough to endure a second childhood of dementia, a stooped back, wrinkles, and no Botox or plastic surgery, I will have a history on my face, and some damn good stories to bear witness that I was here. Just like your children, these stories may or may not live on. I shall bear witness to heartbreak. Children or not, there's no way to escape that.

Romeo still makes me sad . . . poor boy in tights. Timing is everything when it comes to life and death.

The Plus of Child-Less

Cheryl Bricker

I was in Los Feliz back in the twentieth century, walking down the street with my friend Lea to see a film at the fabulous old Vista theater, before the boys from *Swingers* came in and redecorated. We were chatting away about the kind of guy I was likely to end up with (which, according to her, probably wouldn't be my ideal—thanks a lot for *that*, by the way!) as a woman pushing a cart with one hand and walking a dog with the other passed us. In unison, we made a girly, cooing "aaah!" sound. "Oh, what a cutie!" my friend gushed. "So cute!" I replied. "And that was the cutest little outfit," she continued. "What?" I said. Her: "The baby." Me: "What baby?"

I saw the dog—she saw the baby. I didn't even properly identify it as a stroller that the woman was pushing till I glanced back over my shoulder. Sure enough . . . baby. In a buggy . . . and lots of it. Which goes to show you the world we perceive is as individual as the individual perceiving it.

I consciously decided early on (seriously . . . like preteen) that I had other priorities for my future and that adding children to the mix would be impractical and, quite frankly, undesirable. I was never great at fulfilling societal expectations. As a little blonde girl (well, not so little, really . . . I was the tallest girl in my class till sixth grade), people assumed my eyes were blue. They are green. It was expected that little girls, especially little blonde ones, wear pink. To this day it is a color for which I have a certain contempt. And of course, it was assumed I would get married and have babies, or at least "baby." My junior year in high school, I wrote a thesis paper on marriage, citing the historical evidence of women as chattel, laying out a schematic for negotiating various three- to seven-year time frames for marriage contracts based on our biological/cellular and physical/emotional evolution, and, of course, proposing adoption as a solution to our planetary resource depletion and grotesque overpopulation. Pretty much my general life philosophy has been this: if everyone's doing it, there's something suspect about it.

Honestly, I was scared of pregnant women when I was a youth. I remember going to our Midwest state fair and seeing a woman walking toward me who looked—and walked—like she'd swallowed a medicine ball. I broke into a cold sweat and veered into the dairy cow barn to get out of her path, lest the threat that her baby, which was *clearly* overdue, would drop in a goopy heap at my feet and she'd look to me to cut the umbilical cord with some nearby farm tool. I would then promptly pass out, falling face-first into the sanguine mass of placental goo and dirt of the fairgrounds pathway, and spend the next twenty years getting shock therapy to overcome the trauma. I would get equally edgy in elevators when a woman "with child" was a passenger (I already had issues with borderline claustrophobia, but that's another topic). This *agita* was more about having to rise to the occasion and help deliver the baby, kind of like the scene in way too many movies where some ill-equipped buffoon does the same in the back of a cab. So *that* had the double-whammy pressure of channeling some kind of heroic behavior while also trying to overcome an irrational fear of closed-in places. Happily, where I grew up, there weren't many elevators.

Here's what everyone (and when I say "everyone," I mean books geared toward procreation, some of your friends, likely your parents, most of the breeders) would have you think . . . if you eschew having children, you're afraid. Now, I really hate avoiding something because I might be scared of it. This has historically caused me to do some rash things because I suppose I had to prove that I wasn't, indeed, afraid. I had a boyfriend once who, within two weeks of dating, was talking children. It seems I was a desirable genetic match for his vision of his future. I proposed we see if we really even liked each other before engaging in this discussion. He persisted in sneaking in conversations over sushi that were geared toward my feminine fecundity. I told him the fact that he found my uterus sexy wasn't the sexiest thing in the world to me. But after we'd been together a couple months, I started to wonder if I wasn't psychologically misguided on this topic. I allowed some discussion. I pondered the idea that, because of my pregnancy-panic past, I might indeed be scared of having children and not merely making a conscious choice based on personal preference. One night, while sleeping over at his cozy—and when I say "cozy," I mean "little"—house near the beach, I had a dream. Without going into the more revealing aspects that could cause you to analyze things about me that have questionable relation to the topic at hand, I dreamt of an intimate encounter with a previous boyfriend who often starred in "relationship" dreams, where I looked at him and very calmly said, "I don't want to have children, and there's nothing wrong with that." My unconscious voice started screaming, "Wake up, wake up, *wake up!*" until I did. That was sufficient for me. As I lay next to my somnolent, desperate-to-breed boyfriend, I knew my question had been asked and answered. As a footnote, I think it demonstrated real personal growth not to have a baby first and find out if I was scared later.

I admit, the tempting stories of the joys of pregnancy have been great. There was my New York neighbor who had nine *full months* of morning sickness, lying on the cool tiles of her tiny bathroom in our Upper West Side apartment building so her head could be close to the toilet bowl that she hurled into regularly . . . then turned around and got pregnant *again* only to have the same exact nine full months of bathroom dwelling and barfing. There was the recent conversation with a neighbor about her five months of vomiting and constipation, and the cancer drug for nausea they give you that, ironically, makes you more constipated . . . and did I mention, it's a drug for cancer?! I know of a woman who had her lady parts rebuilt in later life because of the giant-domed bundle of joy she pushed from her nether regions. My favorite, and a source of hours of volatile amusement for me, was my girlfriend who was gloriously indignant during the horrifically uncomfortable first half of her pregnancy, routinely saying things like, "You can just bet if fucking men got fucking pregnant there'd be a fucking pill for fucking morning sickness by now!!" I suspect she had a point. In an effort to be helpful, I'd bring her things like sugar-free donuts or some sort of edible item designed for gastric absorption, which would then cause her to howl, "You can just bet if fucking men got fucking constipated . . ."—you get the drift.

The fact is, I never understood nor generally agreed with the reasons people gave me for having children. The idea of creating a "little me" seemed ludicrous and, frankly, really narcissistic. You don't know what you're going to get. As the daughter of a mother who clearly didn't get what she banked on, I know this to be true. And those parents often times are just working out their own disappointments and neuroses on their little cutout doll, passing a more virulent strain of dysfunction into the next generation, in my humble but accurate opinion. Oh, and the continuation of the bloodline, the family name continued (see above: women as chattel)! Well, two abbreviated thoughts: One is I think that's a lame rationale, and two is some bloodlines just need to end. It's been a couple generations past that our ancestors procreated in order to have a crew to farm the land, and, while practical, I don't find it a very nurturing reason, and less than 2 percent of Americans have that excuse now. That god deems the product of any sperm that manages to find its way to an egg and fertilize it is somehow holy *and* that god is anti–birth control is . . . don't get me started. Whatever respect I might have had for the group whose philosophy seems to have become "love the fetus, hate the child" (e.g., deny them health care, take away food stamps, send 'em to wars willy-nilly . . .) has long since dissolved. The only person who ever said anything about having children that remotely made sense to me was my friend Rick—who, by the way, is *sans enfant*—and for the life of me neither of us could remember what it was. That's how rare of an idea it was.

You do get that added extra party or parties (if you're a multiple mother)—the baby shower. I really never liked those parties much. I find participating in the insipid weight or girth-guessing games somewhat insulting to the guest-of-honor, couldn't care less about identifying the puke-colored jars of baby food, and have never much been a fan of the decorations: the mandatory frilly pastels of pinks and blues (remember my aversion to stereotypes), or, in the case of the woman who declines the gender sneak-peak . . . pale yellow. And having to watch the mommy-to-be open and squeal over torturous-looking pump devices and cylindrical poop storage bins . . . well, there are about a hundred other things I'd rather be witness to, including a monster truck show . . . which I've done precisely once and plan on never doing again. The little cute clothes are fun to look at for a while, but let's face it; those things are really all for the bambino. I much preferred the shower that the *Friends* Rachel and Monica gave Phoebe. She was supplied with all the fun and much-deprived gifts she'd want after she'd delivered her brother's triplets (okay, if you weren't a fan, it's too intricate to explain here). Leather pants, tequila, a gym membership . . . all the meaningful and personal things a woman races back to after childbirth.

As a result of being childless, I do get to indulge more of my basic nature—my impulsiveness, spontaneity, self-reflection. I can accept invites for a weekend stay at a friend's lake home, or get the benefit of a last-minute ticket to a show. I can run off to a weekend retreat and participate in omphaloskepsis (look it up). Sometimes a boat excursion around the marina pops up, perhaps some other event that I wouldn't have ferreted out on my own, or an offer to use someone else's frequent flyer miles and go out of town—or country (!)—for a coveted mini-vacation. I don't scramble to find a babysitter or have to reluctantly decline because of a PTA or student disciplinary action meeting, or because I have to go/drive to a soccer/ballet/foot (or any-of-the-balls) game at some ungodly 8:00 AM hour on a Saturday morning . . . which, by the way, I think is *really* unfair to do to the kids, too. Every once in a while, a comparably aged mother-type will say to me, in a tone that implies a nobler, more superior, albeit underappreciated, choice, "I wish *I* could get to the gym once a week! You can just pop off anytime you want, do what you want when you want. You're so lucky!" To that I just smile and reply, "Yep, I am!"

You may think me selfish. Then be thrilled I didn't choose to have kids! Not all of us are willing to spend the time doing the awesome task required in raising another human being. Occasionally, some over-extended, stressed-out friend-parent of mine utters, "You're so smart you didn't have kids." And you know something? They're right. For me, it was smart. Because it's just not accurate—or interesting—to assume everybody's life plan looks the same.

Why I Never Had a Kid

Merrill Markoe

I had the usual amount of fantasies about my future when I was growing up. I remember wanting to be a telephone operator, a child actress, an equestrienne, and someone who ran an employment center, preferably all at the same time. I don't, however, remember having any specific fantasies about being a mother.

No one in my family of origin seemed particularly enamored of that role. Watching my mother on her duly appointed mothering rounds looked to me like nothing so much as such a study in involuntary servitude. My grandmother, who lived with us, didn't seem too excited about the whole thing either. There was never any cooing over babies among the women in my family. If it was their intention to give me the impression that humans under the age of twenty-five were a pain in the ass that could be tolerated but rarely enjoyed, they did their job very well. In fact, the only thing I do recall hearing my mother and my grandmother repeat on a regular basis with regard to raising children was a heartwarming retort that went, "One day you'll have kids of your own and then we'll see how much *you* like it."

Subsequently, I never dreamed of one day having a son or daughter who would talk endlessly about me in therapy, like the other little girls. Instead, by age eleven, my diaries were filled with "I'm never getting married. I'm never having kids."

But I did like the idea of loving and caring for others. So by the time I turned twelve, I had set my sight on getting a dog. As far as I could tell, no one's life became any worse because they were raising an animal. And from the moment I succeeded in making this dream come true, I found everything about the experience to be ten times more fun than had been previously advertised.

Later in life, I went on to wish for pigs and sloths and hedgehogs and echidnas as well as horses, goats, otters, and proboscis monkeys. But somehow I never evolved into someone who wished for more time with my own baby humans.

Maybe this is sad.

When I see how my friends are enjoying the experience of motherhood in all its various stages, it's clear that the women who raised me may have given me a warped message.

At least I gave some serious thought to the idea before biology put a period at the end of that sentence. On the runway to forty, I sat down with therapists and made a concerted effort to dissemble and scrutinize my negative attitude, lest I let my petulant twelve-year-old self make such important decisions for me. But by then, my memory bank was so full of the difficulties I'd experienced spending time with my own family that creating a new one via motherhood still seemed like signing up for another round of holidays and vacations full of unwinnable fights about poor wardrobe choices and badly plucked eyebrows.

"But," every shrink would argue, "you aren't going to have a relationship like that with your own kids! You will do things differently!" To which I'd reply, "Really? Why in the world do you think that? Aren't you the one who explained repetition compulsion to me, wherein a person unconsciously replicates the parent/child dynamic over and over and over?"

The truth is that most of the time, I have no regrets about not passing on my genetic shortcomings to another generation. In fact, I believe that humankind should thank me for my disinclination to replicate. An examination of the life I've lived with my beloved canines offers all the evidence one might need. My dogs, the only creatures on the planet marked by my singular nurturing imprint, have all turned out to be rude and self-absorbed with no respect at all for the rights of others. In all likelihood, if they were children instead of dogs, I would have foisted more Charlie Sheens or Kardashians onto our crumbling culture.

Meanwhile, I go my merry way, committing to successive groups of four canine companions, one after the next. If they have complaints about me, I rarely find out what they are. They don't stop talking to me when I'm grouchy, or bad-mouth me on Twitter. They never initiate lawsuits or try to borrow money. If they think my outfits aren't working, or that I've put on weight, or that the house is looking shabby, they keep it to themselves.

True, they will be no help to me in my dotage. But then neither are a lot of nasty adult children. Rather, my dogs will go to the very end under the impression it all worked out really well between us. Plus, I don't have to go into debt trying to put them all through college. Still seems like a win/win/win proposition all the way around.

Tiny Chocolate Cakes

Susan Norfleet

I'm not a baby person. I never wanted to have babies and, apparently, I never wanted to be one. I know this because every year on my birthday, my mother insists on recounting the story of my birth. She recounts the story of my birth shortly after she laments the fact that I was a month late in coming and she had to suffer through the entire month of July in North Carolina in 1959 when there were no air conditioners and she ate lime sherbet every day, which is why she can no longer stomach the thought of lime sherbet. But she digresses.

"You just didn't want to come out," she says, with a forced smile. "When they brought you in to see me, you could hold your own head up. The nurses couldn't get over it! There you were just looking around the room holding up your own head like you didn't need anybody."

I suppose if you combine that extra month of prep time in the womb with the amazing muscle-developing properties of lime sherbet, the whole thing makes sense.

My mother quickly moves to the story of my tonsillectomy at the age of five.

"I bet you don't remember this, but you had your tonsils out when you were five years old, and I bought you the most beautiful doll. I saved and saved for that doll, and when I gave it to you at the hospital, you started crying. I was devastated! You hated that doll. Do you remember?"

Yes, I do remember. I remember because she tells the story every year and because I had requested an Easy-Bake Oven. It's not that I had any girly inclinations to cook, I just wanted to be able to eat tiny chocolate cakes at my leisure. And yes, I remember hating that doll. It was a big white rubbery thing with fixed eyes and permanently pursed lips, wrapped in a starchy pink dress and matching bonnet. It didn't do anything. It was helpless. It was needy. My mother might as well have given me a sack of pink flour. Then again, a sack of flour would have propelled me closer to my dream of tiny cakes.

For the record, I did eventually have dolls. I had a Major Matt Mason astronaut doll, a Jane West cowgirl doll, and, of course, a G.I. Joe. But in my child's mind, they were not dolls—they were tiny adventurous versions of me. They had spaceships and horses and tanks. Their lives were filled with excitement. They explored new worlds, herded cattle, and tormented my older sister's Barbies. Sissy bonnets were no match for helmets, cowboy hats, and berets. My dolls had careers.

Three children's portraits hang in my mother's hallway. My oldest sister holding a doll. My middle sister holding a doll. Me holding a teddy bear. I was born without a biological clock.

By the time I was in my prime childbearing years, I was too selfish to think about having babies. My twenties were filled with disco nights and upside-down margaritas. My thirties were all about my career. By the time I was in my forties, I was busy undoing what I had done in my twenties and thirties so I could concentrate on what I really wanted to do . . . be selfish. Why would I want children when I could care for helpless, needy dependents through a string of ill-advised romantic relationships?

So here I am in my fifties. Calmer, smarter, and still childless. But while I may be lacking in the maternal instinct department, I am not heartless. It's true that I can sit stoically through a Save the Children ad, but I fall completely apart when Sarah McLachlan sings "Arms of an Angel" for that animal-cruelty campaign. I may not care to peek into your baby stroller, but put a box of kittens in front of me and I become a cooing, babbling idiot.

Every year when my dear mother regales me with the story of me, I am reminded once again that we are who we are from birth. I was never mommy material.

My life has been full and exiting and wonderful. I've traveled the world, had a successful career, and met lots of interesting and famous people. Rarely are they both, by the way. My dream of driving cattle has been realized—and though I've traded my cowboy hat for a riding helmet, I still love galloping around on horseback. I didn't have my own children, but I'm grateful to my sisters for mothering my three beautiful, hilariously funny nephews.

I am well aware that, because of my choices, I may be all alone at the end of my life. My plan is to leave this world as I came in . . . on my own schedule, holding my own head up, and dreaming of the next big adventure and tiny chocolate cakes.

I Kid You Not

Kathryn Rossetter

" I 've never met a woman your age who didn't have children. It's so weird." My forty-year-old lover blurts this out as he rolls off me in ecstasy. Typically not the words a woman wants to hear after a spirited session in bed. Where was the "That was great," or, from his generation, "awesome." How about, "You're so hot," or "so beautiful"? Damn it, at least my vagina is still tight. My breasts almost still perky, no stretch marks. Why is he bringing that up? What the hell kind of spooning is this?

I hate this conversation. I usually try to duck the subject. It's full of assumptions and misunderstandings. Major assumptions are that I am a feminist and career woman who never wanted kids; that I was traumatized as a child; that of course I have had one or more abortions; that I am selfish and self-absorbed and I will never really understand life and the depth of unconditional love. Men assume I'm so independent that I am not even looking for a relationship and am just a good-time girl. Some have even intimated that as a woman I seem "unnatural." I usually just shrug and say, "Life doesn't always work out." I offer no more information. They look confused for a moment and then, thankfully, the discussion stops and I can get on with my life.

The truth is, I always assumed I'd have children. The same way I assumed I'd be married and have a successful career and live almost happily ever after. After all, I was part of a generation of young women who were told we could have it all. No one knew how, but they were sure we could. I never considered myself a feminist. The same way, as I lie next to my buff, younger lover, I don't consider myself a cougar cliché. Sure, as my friends dance at their children's weddings and bounce grandkids on their knees, they squeal and cheer me on in my exploits with my lover. They call me their hero. But I know they don't yearn to be me. They secretly, and in some cases not so secretly, feel sorry for me.

Is my life glamorous or pathetic? Have I not fulfilled my biological imperative? When I die will anyone notice? (Or even miss me until the neighbors complain of the smell?) How did I get here? Dark thoughts as I lie next to my statue of David. But I am Irish. We live for the darkness. We call it poetry. How do I answer my lover? We're not life partners. Of all people, why do I feel the need to tell him my real truth about this issue?

I formulate the words in my head. I was a small-town girl from Pennsylvania; middle class, middle America, middle of the road. Irish Catholic. Dad worked. Mom stayed home with my three brothers and me. We were the American Dream.

I was college educated, but I think my parents just felt that would lead to a better husband with greater income potential. At twenty-three, I married a boy from college. I seemed to be on track with the expected life plan. But I realized early on I had made a mistake. My young husband developed an ulcer and said the stress of dealing with me had given it to him. After three years, we broke up.

My mother comforted and surprised me when she said, "I knew you two were in trouble when he blamed you for his health. That is not fighting fair." Then she also admitted she never thought the marriage would last because she felt I married more out of fear than love. "Why didn't you tell me that? Warn me?" I pleaded. "You would have never listened to me and would probably have resented me for saying it. A mistake isn't fatal. It's an opportunity to learn. You have your whole life ahead of you. And at least you found out before you had children." True, I was still in my twenties, so I had lots of time. "Keep going on with your life," she said. "It will all be all right."

I could always count on my mother to make me feel better. The power she had to calm me down, give me hope, and make me feel safe was a gift. That was motherhood to me, and I dreamt of giving that to my children. I had my father's coloring and sense of humor and my mother's hourglass figure, deep voice, and throaty laugh. I hoped I would develop her wisdom.

I had a dream of being an actress, so, after the divorce, to "get on with my life," I pursued it full throttle. I was on my own, however, as no one I knew had ever made such a risky life choice.

One particularly horrible day, full of rejection, I called home desperate for advice. "I wish I could help you," Mom sighed. "I have no idea what your life is like now. I was married with two children already at your age."

"But Mom, should I quit? Do I have any talent? Should I get a real job? Should I leave New York? Go to L.A.? I don't know what to do."

"Honey, I'm glad I didn't have your options. When I was a young woman, we were only to be wives and mothers or maybe a teacher or a nurse. Sometimes having too many options is paralyzing. You don't make a choice because you assume there is one choice that is perfect or that is 'supposed' to be made. More often it's just trial and error. So keep going, everything will be all right. Call anytime, especially when you have a stomach virus. I know how to help with that." So I kept on.

During this time, the first phase of my college friends were beginning to have their children. Christmas cards were full of baby pictures and tales of how the love of a small child had transformed them. It was a feeling they could never explain and a depth of love they never knew possible. "This is what life is all about. When you have your children, you'll understand." A divide was forming between the mothers and the non-mothers. They were mature Girl Scouts, earning badges in diapers, day care, and competitive potty training, while I remained an immature Brownie, relegated to creating s'mores and making lanyards. We didn't have much to talk about. I was enjoying success in television commercials and working on Broadway with Dustin Hoffman. But my "show biz" friends were delaying having children, so I knew I still had time.

I never had an overwhelming yearning for a child like some of my friends did. They spoke of biological clocks, and their heads twisted off their bodies at the sight of babies on the street. It was like watching men slobber over scantily clad young women as they walked by, except this was a gaggle of grown, educated women reduced to cooing mush at the sight of little babies just lying there doing nothing. I feared something was wrong with me. Whenever I was in a serious relationship, I would feel the strong desire to have a child with that man. I would see us creating new life out of our loving union. But I never felt this when

I was on my own, and during those times, I didn't give children much thought. To be honest, I usually found my friend's parenting skills a little annoying, and their children overly entitled and bratty.

"I tend to agree with you," admitted my mother. "I never liked other peoples' kids. Children can't be your whole life, just a part of your story. (I wondered if she had secretly started reading *Cosmopolitan*.) Be patient. When the time is right, you will be a great mother. Everything will be all right."

True, there was no reason to assume I wouldn't have children. So I kept on going.

My relationships, however, kept ending. I seemed to be on a three-year cycle.

Time passed, and my career was doing nicely. I wasn't a star, but I was a respected, working actress. And, finally, I had a boyfriend who passed the three-year mark. We were happy, and life was in a great place. Most of my "artistic" friends were now getting married and starting their families. Many single women were getting pregnant with sperm donors or friends or adopting because they didn't want to miss out on motherhood. They pushed on me: "Just do it. Get pregnant and he'll marry you. Time is running out if you want a baby."

But the small-town girl in me wanted to be married first. I wanted someone to love me and want to marry me for *me*, not because we'd been together for a while and I got pregnant. I wasn't going to "trap" someone.

Where did this come from? Why did the thought of pregnancy without marriage feel so wrong for me? Irish Catholic strikes again. Intellectually, I supported a woman's right to choose. I held the hands of my friends as they recovered from the procedure. But I knew I could never emotionally survive an abortion myself. So, I was ruthless with my birth control. Birth control was my religion, so I obviously wasn't *that* Catholic.

I suppose it was that I just couldn't wrap my head or my heart around having a child alone. It felt selfish to me. I fulfill my vain desire to have the kid without regard for the life of that child. My financial life wasn't stable. I couldn't just leave food and water on the floor, like for a cat, then hustle around for my income. If it took two to make a child, it seemed logical that it was better for the child's future to have two to raise it. And I still believed a child would be a beautiful extension of our love. Okay, we may divorce, but the relationship had started out from love and commitment.

Admittedly this was an intensely naive, idealistic vision, but, try as I might, I couldn't betray it. As time went by and conversations included new family options, I hid my feelings deeper and deeper. I wished I could embrace the beliefs and philosophies of my friends and colleagues as they carved out and redefined family. They were happy. But if our liberation as women was about honoring ourselves and taking responsibility for our lives, then I had to respect my deep beliefs and myself. Unfortunately, I had no one in whom to confide my thoughts, fears, and sadness. At that time, the women's movement was too fragile to be able to afford the time to support those left confused in its wake. I was a dinosaur, politically incorrect, and alone. So I kept quiet and I kept on.

When my relationship was in year six, my mother got sick and was in intensive care on a respirator. We knew she would live but were afraid she'd die. As she lay there, I sat on the side of her bed and we had the "mother-daughter" talk. Okay, well, it wasn't really fair because she couldn't talk, but it was the best I could do.

"Hey Mom. Nice tracheotomy. When it heals you can get a huge diamond to cover the scar like Elizabeth Taylor did. You know, Mom, I always thought you were June Cleaver. But I was wrong. I never saw you watch a soap opera, you remodeled a kitchen with your bare hands and yet you hated to cook, and I now realize how much strength it took for you to admit you couldn't help me navigate my life. That was such a gift. You released me from needing to "do it right" or in a certain popular way. People say I'm a strong woman. I don't know, but if I am, I got that from you." Her eyes lit up and she nodded her head a little. "I know you worry about me, but I'm okay. Jack and I are going to get married, and he and I want kids right away, so you need to get well because it will be your turn to bore your friends with tales of your grandkids."

She weakly motioned for a pen and paper and struggled to write the following: "Maybe it's best if you don't have children. You never know. At your age they might have two heads." I looked at her and saw the twinkle in her eye, hearing the deep, throaty laugh she was now incapable of making. This was her way of saying it was okay if I didn't have them, and not to do it for her. I was thirty-eight.

A few weeks later my mother died, taking her wit and wisdom with her. She was sixty-three.

A year later I was engaged, buying a co-op, and planning the wedding with my now seven-year boyfriend. I was also planning to stop birth control on the honeymoon. Six weeks before my fortieth birthday and ten before the wedding, my fiancé walked out. He blew the hell out of the white picket fence, my emotional security, and my confidence.

Who was I? What had I done so terribly wrong? Why was I so unlovable? Was I being punished for something? Oh so Catholic. All I could hear was a faint whisper from within, "Just keep on going." *Go where? Do what? Who cares?* I thought. I went to L.A.

Going to L.A. at forty with a broken heart is just slightly less painful than taking a sharp stick in the eye. At that time forty was the new sixty, so personally and professionally, I had a lot of time on my hands. I started coaching my friends for their auditions and discovered I was good at it and enjoyed it. Most of my friends were living a suburban lifestyle: kids in school, SUVs, and soccer. There was no place for me there. I felt excluded from "real life" and profoundly alone. I started running to get in shape and clear my head, and eventually ran back to New York.

Well-meaning friends advocated the Internet for finding men and adoption for having children. With a tinge of pity and relief, women in relationships would say:

"YOU'RE A SMART, BEAUTIFUL, TALENTED WOMAN. WE JUST DON'T UNDERSTAND HOW YOU DON'T HAVE A MAN. YOU MUST BE TOO FUSSY."

"I KNOW SOMEONE. HE'S A LITTLE 'BEEFY,' BUT . . ."

"I'VE GOT A GUY FOR YOU. HIS WIFE JUST DIED. YOU'RE PERFECT BECAUSE HIS KIDS NEED A MOTHER, AND YOU DON'T HAVE ANY SO THERE'S NO COMPETITION."

The dates I went out on were equally inspiring.

"I'M A DOCTOR, BUT I WANT TO ACT."

"I HAD TO LEAVE THE CORPORATE RAT RACE. I'M STUDYING MASSAGE THERAPY."

"I'M VERY LOYAL TO MY WIFE. WE CAN BE DISCREET AND NO ONE GETS HURT."

"ARE YOU STILL FERTILE? I WANT CHILDREN AND I'M LOOKING FOR A WOMAN TO HAVE THEM FOR ME."

As I smiled across the table, inside my head was screaming, "I'm fussy enough to want someone who isn't cheating on his wife, isn't forty pounds overweight, and who works for a living. I don't want to settle for a companion, I want to love and be loved."

In my mid-forties I fell in love one last time. I was giddy and renewed and felt a connection deeper than anything I had felt with my fiancé. I was a late bloomer, I thought, but better late than never. Evidently, though, the connection I felt for him was actually what he was feeling grow between him and his former girlfriend. He returned to her.

I cannot pinpoint the exact moment I realized I would never have children or have the life I'd expected back when I was twenty-three. Somewhere around forty-nine, I had a short, intense affair with my high school boyfriend of all people. (Once a cliché, always a cliché.) When it ended after three months, I threw myself on the bed, and from deep within came a sound like a wolf caught in a trap, howling for its life. I cried for my disappointments, I cried for my mistakes, I cried for my losses. I was a failure as a woman. No one loved me enough to commit to me. I was embarrassed. I felt I needed to apologize for my life. I screamed at God and cried out for my mother. I was not going to "have it all." I cried and cried and my body shook until all I could do was fall asleep.

I didn't wake up for a couple of years. I kept on going, as that was all I knew how to do, but I was invisible to myself and to others. I was profoundly lonely, sad, and tired, and I had lost my hope.

Time heals and aging is unavoidable. My period stopped. I was actually relieved. I felt a chapter close. At some point someone asked me if I missed having children or just the idea of having them. "Well, I never had a root canal, don't miss it," I said in my oh-so-glib way. But it also felt true. I can't miss what I never had.

Slowly, my career evolved into its next phase. I grew as a teaching artist. I now head an MFA acting program at a prestigious university. I touch the lives of about one hundred students every year. Acting is a very intense, personal art form that demands that actors learn self-acceptance in order to relax and become interpreters of human behavior. Teaching it requires that I give them a safe place to fail, help them get back up, and then teach them to go on. In my work I make use of everything I've learned in my life. One day a student said she wanted to grow to be just like me because I'm so "alive and youthful and wise." I laughed and immediately thought, *No, no you don't. You need to aim a little higher.* And then it dawned on me. I fight to get them to honor and accept all aspects of themselves without judgment. The more I help them, the more they have helped me. I nurture them from a different perspective, and I grow daily from the experience. I have found how to share my wit and wisdom.

I have doubted or second-guessed almost every choice I've made in my life: what to eat, where to live, what to wear, who to date, what I should have said, what I should have done. Every choice except one— that I wanted to be married when I had kids. That is the one choice I made and stuck to in my life, and it turned out to be the defining choice of my existence. For it determined that I would journey through life childless. I'm not sorry. I was incapable of any other way.

I will never know what I don't know. I'll never know if there really is a greater love for one's children than I have ever felt. Different, maybe yes. Greater, I'm not so sure. With no children, however, I don't feel that cycle of life in the same way that others do. I never feel my age. I have no constant reminder of what has gone by. That's my ironic silver lining.

I don't see my issues discussed on *The View*. There are no books written, statistics kept, or exposés done on single, childless women of a certain age. My opinions are not sought. I am not even marketed to as a viable consumer. Maybe that's why I feel so compelled to tell my lover the truth of it all. Or maybe he caught me at a vulnerable moment. After all, I am naked. Or maybe I just don't want to be thought of as weird. So, I swallow hard and look deeply into his soft green eyes and confess, "Well, young life never came out from between my legs. So I emulate it now by taking young life in and out from between my legs as often as possible." Out comes my signature laugh. He laughs, climbs on top, and off we go again. My secret is safe; my vulnerability intact. And I can keep going on.

Björn Again

Jennifer Prediger

I'm late.

Gross, if you're thinking what I think you're thinking. For me, that lady train runs with the efficiency of the German high-speed rail system. It's all the other things I'm late for.

I'm an eleventh-hour, last-minute Lucy. I push things to the deadline. As I write this, I can tell I'm going to be late to work. I arrive at the last possible second. To quote a favorite *Real Housewives* dance number, "I'm tardy to the party."

Case in point, this essay was due over a month ago. Ironically, so were my two best friends from high school and college. They were due to have actual babies.

They had them—beautiful, bouncing, little healthy humans. What I had during this time was a little crisis. Like a newborn, it cried out in the night. Then it manifested as my first gray eyebrow hair. It seems my biological clock is ticking, but I'm waiting for the alarm to go off.

As I flipped my uterus over searching for answers to why I wasn't thinking about having children while the two friends I'm closest with were bonding lovingly with their infants, an unbecoming thought popped into my head. What if I have no one to visit me even begrudgingly at the nursing home?

Thankfully I quickly arrived at the conclusion that built-in nursing home guests are not a good enough reason to have children. But speaking of nursing homes, were it possible to skip ahead, I do think I'd make a wonderful grandparent. What's more likely at my pace is I'll be a parent the age of a grandparent, like that sixty-two-year-old lady who posed Demi Moore–style naked and pregnant on the cover of *New York* magazine, though instead of looking like the actress, this woman looked more like a skeleton with a baby bump. A very fertile skeleton, that is.

Lore has it my fertility is falling off a steep cliff this year. I think I turned the magic age where the odds of pregnancy decrease by 50 percent. Then again, that may just be an old wives' tale to get girls like me married off and having babies before it's too late. It does give one pause. Menopause.

No, not yet. But I'm sure I'm starting to sound like a cliché of a selfish person living an extended adolescence in New York City who can't be bothered to have children because she's too busy chasing down other dreams like having health insurance. Well, it may be true, but it's not the only truth. I do know what it's like to raise a child. I've been the parent to my own inner child for quite some time now. Turns out this inner kid thing is hard work. Mine is whiny and expensive. The cost of taking it to therapy alone has been the equivalent of a four-year college.

I could tell you all the other reasons I haven't taken the parenting journey yet—my concerns about the extended economic crisis, overpopulation, peak oil, and not having enough time to take a shower—but that would be slightly misleading. The main reason I haven't had children is the steps I'd have to take to get them. Not love, marriage, then-the-baby-carriage kind of steps, though they matter. I mean the stairs in the New York City subway system. Carrying a stroller up those things is a Sisyphean act. Even if you live in Kentucky and there's only a slight chance you may vacation in Manhattan or its boroughs someday, the prospect of having to lug your baby up those dirty, never-ending stairs is reason enough to abstain from the whole enterprise.

These excuses are pathetic. People who have children are brave and I think maybe better adjusted than I am. I saw a woman on the F train yesterday wearing a well-adjusted BabyBjörn with a little person sleeping in it. Seeing his tiny hand, I considered how nice it would be to have a set of tiny hands of my own. Speaking of the train, reminds me I've got to go get on one. If I leave now, I'll make it to work just in the nick of time. Habits being habits, maybe the kid thing will happen in a similar way. Looking at my watch, I have about six years still to get in the game. Like a player in a sporting event metaphor, I just might get one in at the buzzer.

The Pathology of Motherhood

Valri Bromfield

A proposal for the future edition of the *Diagnostic and Statistical Manual of Mental Disorders* (DSM-5), by Valri Bromfield LPC, MHSP, CBC (Childless by Choice)

Motherhood Personality Disorder, or MPD, is a complex, interfamilial compulsion fueled by estrogen, culture, religion, and the Family Values Industrial Complex.

This disorder is not to be confused with Mental Disorders Due to the General Medical Condition of Pregnancy, which are *always* (despite statements by the Catholic Church) preceded by symptoms of Spontaneous Heterosexual Loss of Cognitive Control, or copulation.

Nor should this be confused with the Impulse Control Disorder known as Entering the Convent. (Please see the Religious and Spiritual category for more information.)

Research findings conclude that most MPD patients sustain sexual relations with their "husbands" for only 2-4 years. Nuns however, receive life-long room, board, religious entertainment and sexual relations. Research shows that this sexual activity is not carried out with their mutual "husband" Jesus, but among the "sisters."

Diagnostic Features

MPD falls under the Cluster D category of overly intrusive/dissociative disorders.

Diagnostic features include:
- Intrusive preoccupation with offspring
- Episodes of major martyrdom
- Intermittent cooking and cleaning

Early Indications

Research suggests that some women later diagnosed with MPD presented indications of the disorder at a very early age. Between the ages of eight and twenty months, the patient begins family or motherhood role-play with dolls. This play can quickly deteriorate into unproductive behavior, such as doll limb amputation, loud hysterical screaming in the doll's face, and full-body doll immolation.

These early practices have been known to lead to unproductive adult mothering techniques later in life, such as forgetting to pick up her four-year-old from day care, introducing her daughter to crack, or making her son dress like George Will to get country club membership. Such behaviors are significant signs that a woman suffers from the disorder.

Course of the Disorder

In the vast majority of cases, the course of MPD leads to persistent toddlers and tiaras syndrome, which will present with the following symptoms:

- Mother's weight gain
- Mother's spontaneous acquisition of an Alabamian accent
- Mother's compulsion to dress the toddler like Kardashian adults
- Tiny, teeny little breast implants that must be "refreshed" at two-year intervals
- Hoarding of anything pink
- Eventual gastric bypass surgery for both mother and child
- Healthy children leaving home by the age of twelve years

In patients presenting these symptoms, be sure to also look for signs of *delusional thinking* in statements she makes, such as, "They'll think we're sisters." In addition, watch for *misdirected maternal libidinal behaviors,* such as engaging in sexual relations with her daughter's high school boyfriend.

If interventions are not instituted at this point, the course of MPD can also lead to *mensa compulsion.* This involves the patient subjecting her child to excessive testing of its intellectual ability, occasionally even with preverbal children. If this testing occurs prior to fourteen months of age, the child should be removed from the home and the mother should be hospitalized at the Betty White Clinic. (Note: Do not confuse this with the Betty Ford Clinic, where mothers go to sober up. The Betty White Clinic is where mothers are sent to loosen up.)

Other compulsive MPD traits include:

- Active and aggressive attachment to the offspring's membership in a college fraternity or sorority
- Occupation preoccupation, e.g.: "My son the reality television show producer."
- Presentation of offspring as merchandise, e.g.: "Look at her, have you ever seen anything so beautiful? Just look at those legs!"

Motherhood Personality Disorder Subtypes

PARANOID TYPE: This type presents in cases where the expectant mother has seen the film *Rosemary's Baby* and clings to the hope that she will give birth to the demon child. (Note: Only diagnose MPD if the delivered baby does not present signs of being the offspring of Satan.)

DISORGANIZED TYPE: This subtype has the greatest impact on the patient's family. From the ages of two to sixteen, the offspring must be transported everywhere by grandparents or other guardians, as the mother is habitually preoccupied with behaviors incompatible with child supervision, such as: an inability to find her car keys, sleeping, watching "her show," or intoxication; or the patient is simply not available, perhaps because she is attending a Zumba Fitness Party or because she flew to Cairo in a manic state earlier that morning.

CATATONIC TYPE: This has been found to be the most adaptive type for the MPD mother with teenagers. The patient lies motionless in bed staring at the ceiling and soiling her clothes, but otherwise does not really give a shit. The patient's children often take advantage of this particular presentation of symptoms, as it facilitates the use of the family home for underage recreational activities, since, when friends' parents later ask if the mother had been present at the time, the juveniles can reply honestly in the affirmative.

Prognosis

With treatment, MPD patients can hopefully achieve partial remission, eventually replacing their child(ren) with several dogs or cats. While personal hygiene suffers with this intervention, the replacement of obsession objects can allow for the eventual reintroduction of human children and grandchildren, *but only under strict supervision.*

In extreme cases, remission is impossible, as with the diagnosis of Mutter Museum Mother, or MMM. In such instances, the mother has undergone excessive elective surgery that has resulted in horrific disfigurement. Unfortunately there is no known cure; this disorder will only remit with the death of the patient. The one bright spot in this particular diagnosis is the benefit of survivors not having to attend to funeral arrangements for their mother once she is deceased, as the museum staff will recover and transport the exhibit immediately upon expiration.

What's It All About, Dudley?

Patricia Scanlon

I don't have any children, and in hindsight, maybe that is as it should be. I'm thinking I may not actually be very good at relating to actual human children. I once had a very short-lived career as a kindergarten teacher. I think that career lasted maybe a week, tops. I got fired, because the children began to cry and hide beneath their desks whenever I sang "Itsy Bitsy Spider" to them. At first, I wasn't sure why. I thought I was doing a good job. I certainly put my all into it, as I do with everything. I spent the entire night, before my first day in the classroom, rehearsing the song and the gestures that accompany it. I wanted to make sure they were precise and meaningful, rather than vague and sloppy, as they so often are. During my training, I had observed other teachers singing the song to their students and their hands would flutter aimlessly while they led the class in song, especially when they got to the bit where the spider falls down the drain. Most of them seemed to just skip right over that part, actually, as if it had never happened. But, in my opinion, isn't that the point of the whole song? Yes, it's true, my rendition of the song did make the children cry and run for cover. Why? I'll tell you what I think, and it's not necessarily a bad thing. I think my interpretation of the song enabled the children to understand, for the very first time, what the song is really all about: a mentally ill spider. Here's this stupid spider, crawls up the water spout, gets washed out by the rain, is given a temporary reprieve by the sun, and she crawls up the very same spout again. Why not try a different spout? The very nature of the song's structure implies this is how this particular spider spends each and every day, crawling up the same spout, knowing full well the rain is going to come down and wash her out of that spout. And yet, the spider continues to do it again and again and again. The definition of insanity, according to Albert Einstein, is doing the same thing over and over and expecting a different result. There you have it; "Itsy Bitsy Spider" is an intrinsically sad song, which I tried to explain to the principal when she fired me for making the children cry while singing, what she called, a simple nursery rhyme.

If I had a child, there would be none of this Itsy Bitsy Spider crap. No, I'd be the lone mother in front of the school marching with a picket sign, chanting, "No more Itsy. No more Bitsy. Stop, stop. With the spout. It's not working. Cut it out." I would be the type of mother that would read Sartre to my children each night before they went to bed, rather than bore them with *Good Night, Moon.* Together, each night, before they fell asleep, my children and I would scale the existential peaks and valleys of Being and Nothingness. Yes, I would be the type of mother that believes you're never too young to start examining your existence. My reasoning: It's better to start questioning things early, just out of the starting gate, before you're too far into the game and there's just no figuring out who the hell you are or why the hell you're here. I would not buy my children silly board games like Chutes and Ladders or Candy Land. How, I ask you, does a game like Candy Land prepare you for the real world, with its Rainbow Trails and Gumdrop Mountains? Have you ever seen a Rainbow Trail or a Gumdrop Mountain? I haven't. So why even put that into a kid's head? It can only lead to confusion and disappointment and more confusion and more disappointment. I would personally design one-of-a-kind board games for my children, games designed to accurately reflect what they could, realistically, expect out of life, games like: Ennui, The Existential Bored Game. Games like . . . oh, crap, let's face it; who am I kidding? I'd be a terrible mother. Actually, that would probably be a more appropriate name for my "bored" game. I ran a few of these thoughts on child-rearing by some of my friends who are parents, and they agreed that perhaps it is better, after all, I don't have any children.

Yes, alas, perhaps my friends are right. I'm also, I admit, very lazy when it comes to homemaking. Well, not so much lazy; it's simply that I would rather be doing something else, anything else. I just don't want to take the time to think about what hamper would go nicely with my shower curtain. Life being short, I use an Albertson's paper bag as a hamper, and when that wears out, I just replace it with another. Who's to say what effect this devil-may-care décor would have had on a child. My own mother wasn't exactly Martha Stewart, but her attempts at homemaking were more charming and whimsical than mine, like something you might expect from a downtrodden bon vivant. For big family gatherings, she'd use an old hubcap as a Jell-O mold and serve the holiday turkey on a plank covered with aluminum foil. All of our walls were half-papered in a haphazard crazy quilt, made from kidney-shaped sections of mismatched wallpaper that my mother would cut out of giant books of wallpaper samples my father brought home from work. "Waste not, want not," she would say. None of the walls ever got finished, as she would only work on them when inspiration hit, which was rarely. My mother's idea of redecorating was to go out and get one of those rugs that comes in a big clear plastic zip bag, lay it down on top of the old one without so much as vacuuming, and then scream, "Come look, everyone! I've redone the living room." The rugs piled up, one upon the other, covering old Cheez-Its and hairpins, never to be seen again. One time, she actually laid a rug over my hamster. We found him a week later. He seemed all right, but he never used his wheel again. I think the incident left him with a bum leg. Their legs are so tiny, it's hard to say. We must have lost at least six inches of height in each of the rooms as my mother "redecorated" over the years, but I think this may have actually ended up being good for my self-esteem, as I've always felt that I am a lot taller than I actually am. I don't know if this was intentional on my mother's part or just a fluke. Either way, I don't think my paper bag hampers would have as profound an effect on the self-esteem of any offspring I may have had.

My husband and I had tried for a number of years, shortly after we got married, in our latish thirties, to conceive. During that time, except for our Batik bedspread and my teddy bear, the bedroom looked like an untidy laboratory. My bedside table became strewn with basal thermometers and a surplus of ovulation kits, their wrappers strewn in a frantic array across the floor. I covered the entire wall in front of our futon with butcher paper, on which I created an elaborate monthly graph, charting my fertility by the hour. Three times a day, like a mad scientist with a sideline in tarot, I would dutifully, and thoroughly, study the elasticity and viscosity of my vaginal secretions, giving them an overall fertility score on a scale of 1 to 10. I would then factor that score into my chances of conceiving at any given hour on that particular day and add the results to the chart, using the appropriately colored Magic Marker. I'll admit, these portraits of fertility did not have the verve and muscular spontaneity of, say, a Pollack. However, if I'd had the foresight to save them, instead of violently tearing them down and throwing them away month after an unsuccessful month, they may have warranted an exhibition in a trendsetting feminist gallery.

Ironically, at a time in our lives that relied heavily on sex for a successful outcome, this was, indeed, not a sexy time for my husband and me. I was becoming haggard and jumpy, not sleeping, up at odd hours, obsessively working on my fertility graphs. As the months passed, I would tear down the old chart and, with the use of a stepladder and my husband's reluctant assistance, cover the entire wall, once again, with a fresh piece of butcher paper. The more we repeated this ritual, the more determined I became to make a baby, while it seemed my husband was becoming just as determined to not make a baby. I began having to lure him onto the futon with promises of back rubs and, when that didn't work, allowing him to keep the women's volleyball game on the TV while he went at it. I consider this a low point, but I was desperate. When he began to lose interest in both the back rubs and the volleyball, I began to beg, to plead, to demand, "Get back in here, you. Make love to me right now, you." I'm sure, to another's eye, God forbid, the sex we were having at that time looked like a mash-up of *The Exorcist* and black-market porn. After my husband had done his part, I would immediately thrust my hips toward the ceiling, looking not unlike Linda Blair. This was my husband's cue to shove a stack of pillows under my ass before shuffling off, looking not unlike the *Exorcist*'s worn-out priest a couple of scenes before he jumps out the window. As he left the room, I would whisper loudly, "Good job."

While I lay with my pelvis thrust in the air, it was understood that I needed to lie silent and uninterrupted for at least a half hour, as prescribed in one of my fertility manuals. During this time, I was supposed to envision our child, my husband's and mine. Let's start calling my husband "Hugh" from here on out, because, well, that's his name. While lying, uncomfortable and contorted, on the enormous stack of pillows, I would close my eyes and envision the best parts of me commingling with the best parts of Hugh. Hugh is a bearish man with a tiny head. Whereas I am reed-thin with a large head. While trying to will a successful implantation into existence, I would envision our two body types successfully combining to create a person whose head would be in perfect proportion with their body. At first glance, you wouldn't notice that Hugh and I had unusual head-to-body ratios. We actually didn't realize it, ourselves, until we tried swapping hats. Really, my head would look much better on Hugh's body and his on mine. When I mentioned this to him, he said, "Yeah, maybe in a horror movie." Fair enough; I can't fault the guy for not wanting to switch heads with me. Hugh is everything I'm not. He is calm and fearless and a one-time *Jeopardy* winner, a man whose emotional pendulum swings steadily between blasé and blas-b. Whereas, mine swings jauntily, on a good day, between hope and despair. And so, often, during this time, while lying silent and still, I would envision the beginnings of a brand-new person, a person whose head sits neither too lightly, nor too heavily, on their shoulders.

After about a year and still no baby, Hugh and I had our respective plumbing checked out. It appeared my uterus was not exactly the Ritz-Carlton I'd thought it was. Also, it turned out that Hugh's sperm had a preference for relaxing rounds of golf over the rigors of football. Between those two revelations, along with our ages, pregnancy without some sort of medical intervention wasn't an imminent possibility.

At the time, Hugh was writing screenplays, while I was doing some film and was sometimes on the verge of becoming a series regular on a sitcom, "sometimes" and "verge" being the operative words. Financially, we were not exactly in the position to bargain with Mother Nature. So, we decided to leave it entirely up to Mother Nature. We chose, unlike the Itsy Bitsy Spider, to cut our losses, emotional and otherwise: no more ovulation kits, basal thermometers, or vaginal secretion readings. Without fanfare, we tore down the last fertility chart, and life moved forward, the way it does. In the back of my mind, not too far back, I thought that perhaps a baby would come along, someday, even though the odds seemed entirely against it. Hugh, on the other hand, was not particularly motivated or driven to have a child, adopted or otherwise, so I decided not to push it.

I eventually came to realize that our bodies were not going to overcome the odds, that a child was not in the picture. Bereaved, I adopted a little black dog who I dubbed Dudley Big Head Little Bear, the Tibetan Wonder Dog of Hope, or Dudley for short. "Tibetan," as we were told by the shelter he was a Lhasa Apso mix, but, it turns out, we later learned, from his groomer, that Dudley was actually a German Monkey Dog, otherwise known as an Affenpinscher. I had selected Dudley from the shelter because when I offered him a bone, he refused it and instead stared into my eyes, as if to say, "That, my friend, is just a temporary fix." When he stood on his haunches, to bore even more deeply into my eyes, he looked like a hairy-faced toddler with a little pot belly and an underbite. There is a painting, actually, done by this guy named Renoir, entitled *Luncheon of the Boating Party,* in which Renoir's future wife, Aline, sits in the foreground holding a little Affenpinscher, while he stands upright on the luncheon table, balanced on his hind legs, with his front paws reaching for Aline's shoulders. If you squint, the little black dog looks remarkably like a small child. Together, Aline and her dog seem blissfully unaware of the others at the party and are the only ones in the painting not engaged in conversation. Although I don't allow my dog to stand on the table, Dudley and I, much like Aline and her Affenpinscher, have formed a unique bond, a bond that has provided me with a much-needed balm.

Is everything as it should be, and has it all turned out for the best? What would be the point of thinking otherwise? Ponder these issues too deeply, and you may look in the mirror and find yourself looking as walleyed as Jean-Paul Sartre. I do, however, think, in my relatively simple way, that maybe, indeed, everything has turned out as it should. For you see, and I hope you will not consider it bragging when I share this intimate fact with you: being a svelte teenager, I used to spend the bulk of my summers running around, carefree, in my string bikini, wearing nothing else but a piece of rawhide wrapped around my ankle. On one of those days, my father called me over to the picnic table and pointed to a couple of tiny brown "blips," as he called them, on either side of my rib cage, just above my stomach, "Good Christ, what's going on there? Have you been bitten? Have you been picking at yourself? Put on some clothes for Christ's sake." Then he pointed them out to my mother, "Dot, take a look at these blips on Patty's stomach, would you? That's what you get for running around wearing nothing more than a couple of Band-Aids." The following week, my mother took me to the doctors to have the blips looked at. I was in the doctor's office for all of two seconds before he reached his diagnosis, "What you've got here is nothing more than a couple of vestigial nipples." He explained this to me as matter-of-factly as he might tell someone they've got a mild summer cold, when, in reality, what he was telling me was: "You've got four boobs." I spent the rest of the day sobbing in my bedroom. And, through the sobs, I heard my mother in the kitchen, laughing on the phone, "Turns out, if Patty ever gives birth, it'll be to a litter." Although

I've never breast-fed my dog, it has crossed my mind, particularly during holidays when the personalized greeting cards begin to pile up, displaying my friends and their cheerful progeny. During this time of year, I'll admit, I've considered sending out a holiday card, too, with a photo of Dudley and me in floppy Santa hats. In the photo, I picture myself staring deeply, and, yes, perhaps a bit walleyed, into the camera. I am wearing a Mona Lisa–like smile, while Dudley lies cradled in my arms, his sweet monkey head pressed against one of my four nipples. Alas, I jest. I have not taken this picture. I do, sometimes, however, curl up in bed with Dudley at night and read him a passage or two from *Goodnight, Moon* before turning out the lights.

About the Editor

Henriette Mantel is a writer/actress/director/producer. She is proud that so many of her friends don't have kids and have lived to write about it.

You can see what she's done in her illustrious career at www.henriette mantel.com. When she was in eighth grade, she came in third in the Vermont State Forestry Essay Contest. Her Emmys for television comedy writing will never compare to that. Her favorite things she has written/directed are the show *In the Middle* (inthemiddleshow.com), *Midge and Buck* (www.icebox.com/archive/index.php?id=show&showid=s8), the documentary *An Unreasonable Man*, and *The Beaver Play*. She grew up in Vermont before it was cool to do so, and she continues to live between there and New York City.

Acknowledgments

Thank you to all my friends, old and new, who contributed their essays to this book. Obviously without you there would be no book. So from the bottom of my heart, thanks. I'm proud to be a writer alongside you, and I'm proud we took on a topic that so many people just want to shove under the rug. If they need to shove this book under the rug, they may—but only after they buy it.

I want to thank my amazing literary agent Lydia Wills and her assistant Nora Spiegel for encouraging me and for selling this book. I love you guys. Thanks to Krista Lyons for believing in it and KJN (Kirsten Janene-Nelson) for your perfectionism, and to everyone at Seal Press: Thanks. Thank you Adriana Trigiani for your help in the very early stages. Thanks soooo much to my assistant Leigh Orsillo. You really really helped me even while you were in the middle of Reality TV sweatshop madness. I appreciate it more than you'll ever know.

A huge thanks to Merrill Markoe for making me laugh when I emailed about how there *has* to be justice in the world and ruthlessly vented about the zillions of women authors on the *Today* show that talk about their goddamn kids!

Thanks to Ellin Baumel, John Richard, Brian Lane Green, Teri Garr, Lew Schneider, Steve Skrovan, Kevin and Kate Meaney, and Mary Ann Halford. And thanks to Francis Gasparini even if I don't know why.

Thanks to Joe Danisi and Stephanie Cannon for asking me to read my essays aloud at the Naked Angels' Tuesday Night Extravaganzas.

Thanks to my friend Nancy Shayne who always encourages me to write from my heart and to Michael Patrick King who championed my first play and always tells me just to write it down and worry about it later. I miss our late nights at the Metaphysical Café on Fifty-Seventh Street.

Thanks to Susan Katz and all the authors who have written the 175,000 self-help books I have read over the years.

I pretty much want to thank everybody I have ever met in my life almost. A special thanks to all the people who have rejected my work of any kind over the years—you are special too in your own way.

Thanks to my friends Andrea Dahlin, Thom Dahlin, Lynn Tierney, and John Slopnick just for being who you are. Thanks to Gayle Richardson Higley, and Karen Croft, too. Thank you Howie and Karen Nielsen for the peace and quiet in Maine so I could finish this.

Thanks to my Aunt Kate who always showed me pictures of her horses and made me understand it was okay not to have kids. Thanks to Uncle Richard for making me, laugh and to Shirley and Paul for all their senior duty.

I want to thank my mom, my sisters Laurie and Chloe, my brother Burk, and my entire family, at least what's left of them. Somehow you manage to let me be me, and for that I am forever grateful. Thanks to my brother-in-law Bill Taylor for all the endless Bruce tickets. Have I mentioned I love Bruce Springsteen?

Most of all thanks to my dad and my brother Jeffrey. You inspire me and help me remember life is short so just get it done.

And a final thanks to my cats, Betty Rainbow and Katrina Kaleena Kightlinger for hanging out with me while I write and helping me keep it all in perspective. But for God's sake, I understand doing things outside the box. You don't need to show me anymore.

—Henriette Mantel
October 15, 2012

About the Contributors

JANETTE BARBER is the host of *Janette's Show* on SiriusXM Stars 107, a spin-off of the very successful *RosieRadio*, of which she was Executive Producer and sidekick. Janette is a stand-up comic, a six-time Emmy-award-winning TV producer and writer, a former TVFN host, and a *USA Today* best-selling author. Janette is Ambassador at Large for Medical Missions for Children (www.mmfc.org), a nonprofit organization that travels to Third World countries to do free surgeries for children with birth defects.

As is the case with many actors, CHERYL BRICKER began writing in self-defense, creating her own opportunity for voice and vehicle. Her one-act play *Catering to Comedy* was first workshopped in New York at the Westbank Theatre, later produced at the Phoenix Theatre Company in Dobbs Ferry, and subsequently appeared at the Lincoln Center Library Theatre. In Los Angeles, she performed her metaphysical fable/comedy *1-800-CALL-GOD* at Arcade. She also penned a scenario for a video game called *Love Resurrected*, as well as a satirical political video encouraging people to get out and vote called *Dr. Cause*. She is currently writing with a partner on a screenplay entitled "Coulda Woulda Shoulda," a coming-of-age crime/romance, a first for the genre. Other projects—screenplays, a novelette, unfinished plays—remain in a drawer. But, liking nothing better than her own opinion, Cheryl has an affinity for this essay format, had fun with it, and was honored to be included.

VALRI BROMFIELD worked as an actor/writer/producer in television and film until she felt she no longer had the intestines for it. Now she is a therapist and loving it. Either way, she has been in therapy all her life.

CINDY CAPONERA, a native Chicagoan, is an actress and writer. She started at the Second City Theater in Chicago, where she performed in the National Touring Company, the E.T.C., and Main Stage, as well as many other local plays. She's written and performed three critically acclaimed solo shows: *Against the Grain; The Debutante Ball,* which appeared at the HBO Comedy Festival in Aspen and was produced for Oxygen Network's Life Out Loud series; and *Cookies and Booze.* Her many television writing/producing credits include NBC's *Saturday Night Live;* Showtime's *Shameless* and *Nurse Jackie;* and Comedy Central's *Strangers with Candy* and *Exit 57.* Cindy has also developed shows for HBO, FOX, Showtime, CBS, and ABC. Her television acting credits include *Sherri, Thick and Thin, Curb Your Enthusiasm, That 70's Show, SNL,* and *Exit 57.* She is looking forward to publishing her first collection of essays: *I Triggered Her Bully . . . Stories from Canaryville and Beyond.*

MARGARET CHO is a multiple-Emmy-and-Grammy-Award-nominated comedian, actress, and singer of Korean heritage known for her edgy, no-holds-barred humor. Having performed stand-up comedy since the age of sixteen, she continues to draw from the primal influence of the eclectic San Francisco neighborhood where she was born. In her early twenties, Margaret received exposure from no less than Jerry Seinfeld, Arsenio Hall, and Bob Hope, which rocketed her into celebrity status and to her own TV sitcom. Since her 1999 acclaimed one-woman show *I'm The One That I Want*, which also spawned a feature film and best-selling book, she has had a string of sold-out tours and successful films. In 2008 Margaret returned to TV on the VH1 reality-sitcom series *The Cho Show*, and in 2009 she joined the cast of *Drop Dead Diva*, airing on Lifetime. In 2010 she self-released the critically acclaimed and Grammy-nominated CD *Cho Dependent*, a funny collection of musical collaborations, on her own Clownery Records. She is currently touring with her latest stand-up show entitled *Mother*. Please visit www.margaretcho.com.

JENNIFER COOLIDGE has been in many movies, TV shows, and plays. In 2010 she was on Broadway in a play titled *Elling*. A certain generation knows her best as Stifler's mom in *American Pie*. Her favorite role ever was playing Charlene, a mental patient who escaped the hospital to fall in love with a beaver and go to Vermont with him to meet his family. She grew up in Massachusetts and now lives in Los Angeles and New Orleans.

BONNIE DATT is a comedy writer and producer, fashion journalist, and, in a former life, an award-winning stand-up comic. Her writing credits span television, print, stage, and the Web and include works for ABC, PBS, USA, Oxygen, MSNBC, Paramount, The Disney Channel, comedycentral.com, msnbc.com, racked.com, and the infamous *Spy* magazine. She is an elected council member of the Writers Guild of America East and has been the Talent Producer and a writer on every WGAE Awards show since 2009. A native of Cleveland, Ohio, Bonnie graduated summa cum laude from New York University and went on to graduate studies at the University of Pennsylvania's Annenberg School for Communication. Bonnie and her wonderful husband, Chris, are very happy with their child-free status, although Bonnie has been known to occasionally anthropomorphize stuffed animals and house plants.

JEANNE DORSEY is a playwright and author of *Footprints in the Snow*, a play about a couple who adopt a troubled eight-year-old Russian boy. The play developed at New York's Naked Angels' Tuesdays@9 weekly reading series and the Ensemble Studio Theatre Playwrights Unit, where she is a member. Her play *Blood from a Stoner* was produced last spring in the 2009 Ensemble Studio Theatre Marathon.

NORA DUNN's first job in front of a camera was with *Saturday Night Live*. Other TV credits include NBC's drama *Sisters*, Fran Drescher's sitcom *The Nanny*, HBO's *Entourage* as Dr. Markus, as well as *Boston Legal*, *Criminal Minds*, *CSI: Miami*, *Curb Your Enthusiasm*, *Don't Trust the B----In Apartment 23*, *It's Always Sunny In Philadelphia*, *Harry's Law*, *Law & Order*, *Numb3rs*, *Psych*, *Pushing Daisies*, and *The X-Files: Wonderland Parts I & II*. Film credits include *Bruce Almighty*, *Bulworth*, *Drop Dead Gorgeous*, *It's Complicated*, *Laws of Attraction*, *Miami Blues*, *Pineapple Express*, *Runaway Jury*, *Three Kings*, *Working Girl*, *Zoolander*, and *Guilt Trip* with Seth Rogan and Barbra Streisand. She published a collection of comedic stories, *Nobody's Rib*, with HarperCollins. Theatrical performances include Nora Ephron's *Love, Loss and What I Wore*, Eve Ensler's *The Vagina Monologues*, and George Furth's *Precious Sons*. Her critically acclaimed one-woman show, *Small Prey*, ran for sixteen weeks in Los Angeles. Her new one-woman show, *Mythical Proportions*, opens in 2013 in Chicago, her hometown.

JANE GENNARO is famous for her talent and versatility as an artist, writer, and performer with an eclectic array of accomplishments that include being a commentator on NPR (National Public Radio), a playwright at The American Place Theatre, and an exhibiting artist at the Fashion Institute of Technology. She lives in New York City and upstate New York with her sexy husband who loves to cook.

LAURIE GRAFF is a writer living in New York City. Her novels include the bestselling *You Have to Kiss a Lot of Frogs, Looking for Mr. Goodfrog*, and *The Shiksa Syndrome*. She's a contributor to *The New York Times* Complaint Box, *Live Alone and Like It, It's a Wonderful Lie*, and *Scenes from a Holiday*, and has penned several short plays and published monologues. Visit her on Facebook or at www.lauriegraff.com.

JULIE HALSTON is one of the theater's busiest actresses and comediennes. She just finished costarring on Broadway in the Tony Award–winning musical *Anything Goes*. Her performances have garnered her three Drama Desk Nominations, two Outer Critics Nominations, and two Drama League Nominations. Her range and résumé include costarring on Broadway with Alec Baldwin and Anne Heche in *The Twentieth Century* to her acclaimed performance as Bitsy Von Muffling on the smash TV show *Sex and The City*. She cofounded the legendary off Broadway theater company Theatre-in-Limbo with playwright Charles Busch and received the prestigious Legend of Off Broadway Award from the Off Broadway Alliance. Her sold-out one-woman show *Classical Julie* has been extended five times at the legendary Birdland Jazz Club, and she will be back there in the spring of 2013. Her book *Monologues for Show-Offs*, which she wrote with friend Donna Daley, is now used as a standard text by colleges, casting agents, and performers in all media. Julie and Donna are currently adapting their success with this book into a play. Miss Halston lives in New York with her husband, Ralph Howard, the anchorman for Howard Stern's *Howard 100* News Department on SiriusXM Radio.

DEBBIE KASPER is a two-time Emmy-nominated TV writer and award-winning producer/writer/performer, as well as a director, actress, stand-up comic, and international humor author. She's toured America several times over, either as a stand-up comic or a writer/performer with one of her many theatrical shows, entertaining America one hit at a time. Her one-woman show *Without Me My Show is Nothing* won the DramaLogue award as best solo show in L.A. Her two-woman show *Self Help The Comedy* toured America for several years, earning rave reviews. Her show *BoomerMania: The Musical About the Baby Boomers*, which she cowrote, codirected, and coproduced, is currently touring America. She will soon be performing/touring her new parody *Zelda Bing's Love Camp*. Always darlings of the press, Debbie's shows have been called "masterpieces," "hilarious," and "hysterical" in dozens of national papers. Whether in NYC, L.A., or criss-crossing the country in between, Debbie has been making people laugh for several decades. Visit www.debbiekasper.com.

SUE KOLINSKY started her comedy career as a waitress in New York City. After getting fired for a cynical remark to a customer, she decided to take her humor somewhere it would be better appreciated . . . The Original Improvisation. And it was. For the past twenty years, audiences have appreciated Sue all across the country. Her comedy skills also landed her a job as the original host of Short Attention Span Theater on Comedy Central. Other TV appearances include *The Tonight Show, Comic Strip Live,* two comedy specials for Lifetime, and *Bob Hope's Young Comedian's Special* on NBC. She has written for the WB show, *Brotherly Love,* HBO's *Sex and the City,* and *The Ellen Show.* She also had a morning talk radio show, *Mason and Kolinsky,* on WNEW in NYC. She cut her teeth as a producer on *The Osbournes,* and for the past three years she's produced *Top Chef,* garnering two Emmy nominations.

MAUREEN LANGAN is an award-winning comic and broadcast journalist. She headlines at clubs and theaters throughout the United States and has been featured at festivals in Ireland, Canada, and England. She's appeared on HBO, FOX (sorry), *ABC News, CBS This Morning, Comics Unleashed, The Joy Behar Show,* the Paramount Pictures film *Marci X,* and in many national commercials. She hosts a weekly talk show on KGO Radio in San Francisco. Maureen lives in New York City and Los Altos, California. She grew up in Lake Hiawatha, New Jersey, where there is no lake.

BETH LAPIDES is the host and creator of Un-Cabaret, which she has produced since 1993 as a live show and for Comedy Central, Comedy World Radio, and Amazon VOD. She has hosted a daily radio show, *The Beth Lapides Experience,* on Comedy World Radio as well as the series *The Other Network* and *Say The Word.* She's been on NPR's *All Things Considered, Politically Incorrect,* ABC Radio, and HuffPo. As an actress she plays offbeat authority figures, most notably on *Sex and the City.* Beth is the author of *Did I Wake You? Haiku for Modern Living* and has written for *O, The Oprah Magazine, Los Angeles Times,* and *Elle Decor;* her monthly column, "My Other Car Is a Yoga Mat," was syndicated by *LA Yoga* magazine. She teaches The Comedian's Way workshops at Kripalu Center for Yoga and Health. She has written and performed numerous shows, including her most recent show, *100% Happy 88% of the Time.*

WENDY LIEBMAN has been a regular on late-night television, including Carson, Fallon, Letterman, Kimmel, Ferguson, and Leno. She has done half-hour specials for HBO and Comedy Central, and her first hour, *Wendy Liebman Taller on TV,* premiered on Showtime. Wendy has been in two documentaries: *The Aristocrats* and *The Boys: The Sherman Brothers' Story,* and she was the recipient of the American Comedy Award for Best Female Comedian. Wendy currently cohosts *Unbound* with Terri Nunn on KCSN, 88.5 FM, in Los Angeles, and writes *LMAO with Wendy,* a blog about health (because if you can't do, teach)! She was also recently #23 Down in *The New York Times Magazine* crossword puzzle. Wendy performs at clubs, corporations, and benefit shows throughout the U.S. and Canada, and she lives in Los Angeles with her husband, Jeffrey Sherman, her amazing stepsons, and her two funny dogs.

BERNADETTE LUCKETT is from Berkeley, California. She discovered her talent for writing when she won first place in the *Oakland Tribune*'s Aunt Elsie's Story Contest at the age of eight. As a teenager, she wrote beautiful yet extremely depressing poetry and was published in a national poetry anthology. She graduated from San Francisco State University with a degree in biology, and she has worked as a lab tech in a VD clinic, a model with the Wilhelmina Agency New York, a cookie packer at Langendorf Bakery, a stand-up comedian, and a producer/writer on several sitcoms. Bernadette recently cowrote *21 Days of Enlightenments,* a fun, interactive workbook aimed at pushing people past their comfort zones. She occasionally posts stories and poems on her blog, *Stuff Bernadette Wrote* at www.stuffbernadettewrote.blogspot.com.

MERRILL MARKOE is an Emmy-award-winning humorist and author of eight hopefully funny books. Her most recent collection of short pieces, now in paperback, is called *Cool, Calm, and Contentious.* You can find out more than you needed to know about her on her website merrillmarkoe.com. She is also on Facebook and Twitter.

ANDREA CARLA MICHAELS is a storyteller, former Los Angeles stand-up comic, and game show writer who now names companies and products for a living as the founder and sole employee of ACME Naming. Andrea has written for *Designing Women* and has created dozens of crossword puzzles for *The New York Times,* the *Los Angeles Times, TV Guide,* and *The Wall Street Journal.* She spent her most memorable years as a chaperone for *The All New Dating Game.* Andrea loves playing/teaching Scrabble, learning languages, and traveling (when her cat allows). The highlight of her life, thus far, was winning a motorhome on *Wheel of Fortune* (actually, that highlight is now tied with petting a kangaroo outside Brisbane). Though she grew up in Minneapolis, Andrea has resided in San Francisco for the last two decades and is mother to no one.

VANDA MIKOLOSKI has been making money being funny since 1981. She has worked in all fifty states and a few foreign countries. She lives in Venice, California, with her ideas and stories and things. She loves all her girlfriends, many of whom are in this book, very very much.

JUDY MORGAN, a native Chicagoan, was trained in improvisational theater and performed for three years with Second City's resident company. Using skills learned though improvisation—observe, recreate, inform, entertain—she has written for stage, radio, television, and film. Feeling the need for change, Morgan now lives in Texas and divides her time between the Piney Woods in the east and the high desert in the west. She writes nonfiction, a genre defined by what it is not. She has been recognized by the Texas Associated Press Managing Editors with their Comments and Criticism Award.

Before moving to Maine twenty years ago, JUDY NIELSEN was involved in improvisation and theater in Chicago, New York, and Canada. She was a member of Inanna, Sisters in Rhythm, as a musician for ten years, and she has written and performed two solo shows: *Mother Tongue* and *Living in a Body*. Judy lives in Whitefield, Maine, where she teaches T'ai Chi Ch'uan, djembe drumming, and meditation.

SUSAN NORFLEET is a former actor and stand-up comedian whose credits include a long list of TV shows and movies that are so old they are no longer being shown late at night on obscure cable stations. She currently lives in upstate New York, where she splits her time renovating old houses, Googling information about hot flashes, and trying to figure out how to delete herself from Facebook. She has not updated her website in five years, so please do not plan to attend anything listed there as an upcoming performance. Most recently she had the good sense to fall in love with a chiropractor and is living virtually pain free with her partner, two cats, and two horses.

SUZANNE O'NEIL has spent the bulk of her life being chased by the villagers, who haven't caught her yet. At present she is either holed up in a deserted windmill in the Transylvanian countryside or skulking the outskirts of Talbot Manor and wondering why Larry Talbot always wears dark shirts and a light suit. This is what happens when one peaks at age three.

JENNIFER PREDIGER is an actor and video journalist currently living above the loudest intersection in the East Village. The noise helps her avoid hearing the increasingly loud grinding of her own biological clock.

KATHRYN ROSSETTER is an actress, writer, and teacher. She was born and raised in Pennsylvania with three brothers and attended Gettysburg College. She has performed on and off Broadway, on film, on television, and in cabaret. She teaches acting and is currently Head of the Acting Department in the MFA program at The New School for Drama in New York City. She also does executive coaching for speaking and presentation skills. She has three nieces and two nephews and lives in Manhattan with her Chihuahua, Rambo.

A former staff writer for *Roseanne* and *Saturday Night Special*, BETSY SALKIND is the author of two children's books for adults: *More Than Once Upon a Time* and *Betsy's Sunday School Bible Classics*. After earning her master's degree at MIT's Sloan School of Management, she worked briefly as a Federal Reserve Bank examiner but left in her mid-twenties to pursue a career in stand-up comedy. Best known as "Squirrel Lady," Betsy has appeared on *The Tonight Show with Jay Leno* and Showtime's *Fierce Funny Women*. She also wrote and performed the one-woman satire *Anne Frank Superstar*. In her spare time Betsy has lobbied and organized for the National Association to Protect Children and was instrumental in changing California law to offer equal protection to children who have been sexually abused by family members. Visit www.betsysalkind.com.

PATRICIA SCANLON is a writer and actor who splits her time between Los Angeles and New York.

JEANETTE SCHWABA VIGNE likes to write about normal, everyday things like loving relationships with suspected manic-depressives; living with terrorists/freedom fighters; and pretending to look for work in the worst U.S. economy since the Great Depression. She's currently writing/performing a story cycle about her adventures in Ireland, which is probably morphing into a novel. On the page, and in acting the story, she brings her characters vividly, and hilariously, to life.

NANCY SHAYNE wrote the book, music, and lyrics for *Marcy in the Galaxy,* produced by Transport Group in NYC. She contributed music, lyrics, and stories for *The Audience* (nominated for Best Musical, Drama Desk Awards–NYC). She wrote incidental music for the last two seasons of *Sex and the City* and most recently wrote with Mark Berman the theme song for Henriette Mantel and Kevin Meaney's web series *In the Middle* (inthemiddleshow.com). Once upon a time she was the musical director for Chicago's The Second City (Touring Company) and one of the founders of Detroit's Attic Theatre. She is most proud of her one-act musical *Two Bitter Women in a Coffee Shop,* which premiered at the Aspen HBO Comedy Festival. And in another life, she performed for years as a stand-up comedienne and still makes herself laugh. Currently she is working on a new musical and a book.

CAROL SISKIND started her stand-up career in New York, where she honed her skills in all the comedy clubs in the City. She then moved to Los Angeles, where she appeared on network television shows, including *The Tonight Show* with both Johnny Carson and Jay Leno. She was a regular on FOX's *Comic Strip Live* and *Sunday Comics,* where she wrote and performed a series of personal film pieces. She's been on two Showtime specials and hosted a segment of Lifetime's *Girls' Night Out.* She's infinitely proud to have appeared on HBO's *Larry Sanders* on an episode she pitched to Gary Shandling. Nominated for Best Female Club Comedian by the American Comedy Awards, Carol has headlined clubs and theaters throughout the United States, England, and South Africa. From L.A. she moved to Las Vegas, Nevada, where she worked every major hotel/casino in town. You may have read about Carol in *People, Newsweek, Mademoiselle, The New York Times, The Sunday Times* of London, and *The New York Times Sunday Magazine,* where she appeared on the cover. She's thrilled to be living back in New York City, her home and never-ending source of creative inspiration.

ANN SLICHTER lives in Los Angeles and has written for such television shows as *The Megan Mullally Show, Win Ben Stein's Money, Are You Smarter Than a Fifth Grader?* and *Rhoda.* (Okay, not the last one.) She's available for a great relationship with the right available man, including your single brother or newly divorced neighbor.

TRACY SMITH kicked off her career in stand-up comedy in 1989 by winning an amateur contest at the Washington/Dulles Airport Holiday Inn. Soon after, she moved to New

York and then Los Angeles, which was all just as the brochure said it would be. She has appeared in many prestigious festivals, including Montreal's Just for Laughs; she has had development deals with several major networks and studios; she has written for Spike TV's animated series *This Just In;* and, among her many television milestones, Tracy has a half-hour special on Comedy Central, as well as a one-hour special on The Comedy Network. She was listed in *Variety* magazine as one of the Top Ten Comics to Watch, and the *Los Angeles Times* says Tracy is "Blonde and buxom with material as tight as her skirt." Tracy currently lives in Raleigh, North Carolina, with her dog, Betty, from where she continues to headline venues all over the continent.

AMY STILLER is an actress and comedian who has been seen in film and television, regional and New York theater. She has also written her own comedy that she performs from time to time in coffee houses all over the place. Characters are her speciality. She is also in the book *Dirty Laundry: Real Life. Real Stories. Real Funny,* edited by Maggie Rowe and Anderson Gabrych. This is her second published essay. She lives in New York City and Los Angeles. She can be found at www.amystiller.com.

SUZY SORO is a comedian, actor, and writer. On *Seinfeld* she got the last chocolate babka, and on *Curb Your Enthusiasm* Larry David called her a very bad name. Her first memoir, *Celebrity sTalker,* was published in 2012. She lives in Los Angeles, waiting for the next earthquake to destroy her enemies. Come to www.WhereHotComesToDie.com or follow her on Twitter @hotcomestodie.

Writer-actress NANCY VAN IDERSTINE's film roles include *The Seller, The Last War Crime,* and *Slowdown.* She has provided voice work in various animated programs, including starring as Mama Chu in 2011's *Little Big Panda,* as the shape-shifting Impostra in the *Power Rangers* series and films, and on hundreds of audio books. On stage, her HBO Workspace original one-act *7 Years I Could Have Spent in Vermont* found an enthused standing-room-only audience who bought her snacks after the show. Nancy's thoughts appear in blog form at theme.wordpress.com/credits/gentleroar.com. She has also written hundreds of specialty pieces for film studios. Her first book, *Twentieth Century Fox: The First 75 Years,* sold exclusively with a collection of the studio's best seventy-five films at a retail cost of around $500. Her books *Vegan & Gluten-Free Recipes To Live For* and *Really Bad Sex: How Not To Seduce A Woman* can be found online for considerably less. Visit www.nancyvaniderstine.com.

Notes

CHAPTER 3: WHAT TO EXPECT WHEN YOU'RE NEVER EXPECTING

[1] *The Boy in the Plastic Bubble* was a seventies' TV movie about a sick teenager who lived a shut-off existence. It starred a young John Travolta—in his pre-alleged "massages with happy endings" days.

[2] This description was approved by Chris.

[3] The repetition of this description was also approved by Chris.

CHAPTER 12: CALL ME PECULIAR—YOU WON'T BE THE FIRST

[1] The only walk I took down *that* aisle was in late 2001, when I carried to the altar for his funeral the cask containing the ashes of my morbidly obese brother who had dropped dead in front of a thinner brother's Christmas tree on Christmas Day. Despite my paralyzing grief, this irony was not lost on me.

[2] Norman Bates owned the Bates Hotel in Alfred Hitchcock's *Psycho*. He was not a nice guy. A kid like this is not what is ever intended.

[3] *All* Children over age five are fascists. They have to be, or they'll never learn to tie their shoes, tell time, or learn grammar. Oh, wait—schools stopped teaching grammar to children based on the belief that it was fascistic—*another* reason to not want children.

[4] Charles Laughton starred as the hunchback Quasimodo in the film *The Hunchback of Notre Dame.*

[5] After rereading this I realize I'm more selfish than Ayn Rand. If you don't believe me, just look and see how many of my paragraphs start with "I."

CHAPTER 21: WHY I DIDN'T HAVE ANY CHILDREN THIS SUMMER

[1] Both the multiples phenomenon and "quiverfull" hyperfertility seem to be a First World obsession; many women with large families in developing countries—and some parts of the U.S. again—very much want contraception, which is not available to them, for economic and more often for political reasons.

CHAPTER 29: BEARING IT

[1] I can't have children according to my lease.

I want to be a mother. I've been called one.

You have to have safe sex because you could get something terminal. Like a kid.

I once thought about freezing my eggs, but only if I could also freeze this really great babysitter I know.

My mother said that when you have children you give up things, like your will to live.

I don't want to be pregnant. I don't want to have to share my food with anyone.

My ex-boyfriend wanted children because he wanted more friends.

I'm very immature for my age, according to my pediatrician. He's a double stupid-head.

I am past my sexual peak and my credit limit.

If I ever had kids I would definitely breastfeed them. Because I don't know how to cook.

2 Steve Trilling, circa 1984, Play It Again Sams

3 For the record, I am not comparing having a baby to getting a spike through your head, because, as stated above, absolutely nothing compares to either one of these experiences.

Selected Titles From Seal Press

Two Is Enough: A Couple's Guide to Living Childless by Choice, by Laura S. Scott. $16.95, 978-1-58005-263-4. Childless by Choice Project founder Laura S. Scott explores the assumptions surrounding childrearing and the reasons many couples are choosing to forgo this experience.

No Excuses: 9 Ways Women Can Change How We Think about Power, by Gloria Feldt. $18.00, 978-1-58005-388-4. From the boardroom to the bedroom, public office to personal relationships, feminist icon Gloria Feldt offers women the tools they need to walk through the doors of opportunity and achieve parity with men.

Single State of the Union: Single Women Speak Out on Life, Love, and the Pursuit of Happiness, edited by Diane Mapes. $14.95, 978-1-58005-202-3. Written by an impressive roster of single (and some formerly single) women, this collection portrays single women as individuals whose lives extend well beyond Match.com and Manolo Blahniks.

Gawky: Tales of an Extra Long Awkward Phase, by Margot Leitman. $16.00, 978-1-58005-478-2. Tall girl Margot Leitman's memoir is a hilarious celebration of growing up gangly, a cathartic release of everything awkward girls are forced to endure, and a tribute to a youth that was larger than life.

Dancing at the Shame Prom: Sharing the Stories That Kept Us Small, edited by Amy Ferris and Hollye Dexter. $15.00, 978-1-58005-416-4. A collection of funny, sad, poignant, miraculous, life-changing, and jaw-dropping secrets for readers to gawk at, empathize with, and laugh about—in the hopes that they will be inspired to share their secret burdens as well.

Undecided: How to Ditch the Endless Quest for Perfect and Find the Career—and Life—That's Right for You, by Barbara Kelley and Shannon Kelley. $16.95, 978-1-58005-341-9. Mother and daughter Barbara and Shannon Kelley explore how women's choices have evolved, why it's so overwhelming, and what we can do about it—starting with a serious shift in perspective.

Find Seal Press Online
www.SealPress.com
www.Facebook.com/SealPress
Twitter: @SealPress